To Ben & Pats
The hunting so
delicious. The vin
was exciting. I'm a
You're wonderful.
Best wishes!

Also by Alan Liere

Bear Heads and Fish Tales

. . . and pandemonium rained . . .

By Alan Liere

Cover Design and Illustration
By A.J. Weir

Inside Art
By A.J. Weir

Page Layout and Typography
By Charles B. Summers
Pacific Publication Services
P. O. Box H
South Bend, WA 98586

Publisher
Pease Mountain Publications
P.O. Box 216
Deer Park, WA 99006

For information or orders contact:
Pease Mountain Publications
P.O. Box 216
Deer Park, WA 99006

Library of Congress Cataloging in Publication Data:
Liere, Alan W.
. . .and pandemonium rained

1.Hunting—Ancedotes, facetiae, satire, etc.
2.Fishing—Ancedotes, facetiae, satire, etc.

ISBN: 0-9652697-0-1
LCCN: 96-92318

Printed in United States of America

Dedication

To Mom and Dad

Table of Contents

Pease
Mountain
PUBLICATIONS

Author's note

When I was a kid, I read a whole bunch—mostly books about dogs and horses and mountain men and Indian chiefs, but a lot of outdoor magazines, too. On a hot summer afternoon, you could often find me belly-down on a blanket in the shade of our house, methodically devouring whatever treasures I had found that day in the county library. It would be years before I would slip two paper shells into an old double-barreled Baker shotgun and set out to ambush a pheasant on my uncle's Columbia Basin ranch, but I liked to read hunting stories. It would be years before I tried anything more adventurous than grasshoppers on a farm pond for bluegill, but I liked to read about exotic destinations, dry flies, muskie plugs, and all sorts of wonderful tales in which my fishermen and hunter heroes just barely came out on top.

In comparison, I suppose the hook and bullet writers of today are a lot more sophisticated than those I was reading in the 50s. In *MY* magazines, stories pretty much started and ended the same: the sportsman got wind of a particularly large trout or particularly ferocious and vindictive grizzly, went looking for it, suffered many disappointments, persevered, and then found his quarry just minutes before last light on the final day of the season. With no time to lose, he snuck into position, his heart pounding through his shirt, sweat pouring into his eyes, his hands trembling. Indeed, *MY* heroes were a messy, human sort.

Then—the predictable moment of truth. The cast was made, the arrow released, the trigger pulled **". . .and pandemonium reigned."** That's what happened every single time! But I was a kid, and I didn't know about homonyms, and I thought the writers meant "**rained**." I could just imagine that pandemonium falling from the sky and soaking everyone with big, wet, drops of delightful-sweet chaos. And that was the part I was waiting for, and it's still the image I prefer. I love it when that pandemonium gets in there and rains all over the place. And it's a good thing, too, for pandemonium is the essence of what I am.

So, is this book predictable? Definitely not.

Does pandemonium rain/reign? Constantly.

Is this a hunting and fishing book? That and a lot more; it's an accumulation of outdoor love stories in which no one gets hurt much and no one gets pregnant. Not even a little. This one embodies the illusory blend of truth, beauty, and lunacy that is my life. Your life, too. Just see if you don't agree.

Alan Liere
Loon Lake, Washington

Introduction

Editor types, especially those who work for outdoor-oriented magazines, are a sorry lot. "Ink-stained wretches" is how Robert Ruark, a wonderful writer from another generation, put it. We spend the majority of our waking hours in small rooms in the bowels of big cities, hunched in front of a computer screen or in a puddle of desklamp light, reading and revising and rewriting, wishing we were out there in the big outside, doing all the neat things that pulse from the pages of the copy we work on.

Every so often, though, our drab existence is brightened by the likes of Alan Liere. During my 18 years as editor of AMERICAN FORESTS, staffers were occasionally drawn to my office to find out what was causing the sounds ranging from strangled snickers to outbursts of loud laughter. Usually, they found me reading a Liere opus. I'd quote a passage out of context, and they'd stare blankly at me or leave the room quietly. His stuff is like that—you have to have been there and done that, or at least braved one of his zany essays all the way to the end.

Now, I won't say that I myself have ever eaten porcupine meatloaf, or detonated a cowpie with a firecracker, or been called a hairy vetch, or worn a sow-pig outfit while cutting firewood. But, like Liere, I have released a wall-hanger fish to prove my inherent good sportsmanship, dug clams in mud up to my knees, kept fishbait and deer skins behind the seat of my truck for years, and suffered bouts of the heretofore unrecognized malady known as The Coyote Reflex.

Big Al's humor is not for everyone. I would not, for example, read one of the book's chapters to an evening gathering of the Los Angeles literati. The Smithsonian Institute is not clamoring to enshrine Liere in one of its many museums. But you'll find this tome to be terrific armchair tonic if you are the sort of person who'll never model underwear, who has missed 179 grouse in a row, dropped a tree on his chainsaw, and is losing his hair and his hearing simultaneously. Liere says he is reaching the time of life in which he can boast of "the auditory discrimination of a railroad tie." Yeah, Al, I hear you—but not very well.

This guy has been stuck, lost, and maltreated in an amazing variety of outdoor paradises. His tales are peopled by an equally diverse cast of characters, ranging from JuJu Perdicious (don't trim Christmas trees with him) to Aunt Doreen (don't take her fishing) to my personal favorite, Thayer the Abnormal—everyman's brother-in-law.

Liere may well have, as he says somewhere in here, "a congenital exigency to be aberrant." But unless I miss my guess—or unless you're wound way too tight—you'll find in this book something far more substantial than an aberrant nature. You'll find a piece of your own persona that you'd like to express a whole lot more than you do—a free and congenial spirit that is most likely to get footloose during a trip into the big outside. A part of you that is genuinely happy and fulfilled.

Bill Rooney
Manassas, Virginia
Former Managing Editor,
OUTDOOR LIFE, and Editor, *AMERICAN FORESTS*

They're hanging from a tree in Texas

Long before disposables became popular, I invented disposable eye glasses. They weren't supposed to be, and their replacements have been expensive, but a ritual which began in 1952 with a pair of eight–pound black horn rims continues today, nevertheless. Since age eight when I permanently misplaced that first hateful pair, I have resigned some 100 sets of spectacles to lonesome obscurity. Largely, this is due to the fact that as I evolved as an outdoor sportsman, I found more places to lose things; my annual replacement costs have doubled, tripled, and even homered, causing my poor wife all sorts of monetary grief and some gastric distress besides. More than once, I have heard her tell people I funded my opticians ski condominium, as well as his mother's hip replacement. This is ridiculous. It was his mother's knee cap, and he probably would have built the condominium anyway.

I tried contact lenses once but flushed them down the toilet for reasons I prefer not to discuss. Suffice to say the act was intentional and I was not, as some people have suggested, washing my hair. Today I wear expensive bifocals, but despite the fact Dad is no longer footing the bill, I am still unable to keep a pair longer than six months—which is, incidentally, a personal best.

Eye glasses, you see, have just never felt right on me, and while I am forever taking them off, and *do* have some favorite spots for them in the house, once I get outside, all bets are off. My wife, Lacey, says if I could tote the refrigerator or the TV along on my trips afield, I would have a reasonable chance of finding my glasses on top when I need them. As it is, however, I am just as likely to fling them overboard when a good bass hits, or lay them on the pickup tailgate while loading the boat. Later, I will have no idea where, when, or why I removed my specs, and will, in fact, often go several hours before making the connection between my headache and the fact I'm not wearing glasses anymore. On a rafting/fishing excursion just last year, I went a day and a half before realizing my glasses were somewhere on the bottom of a 12–mile stretch of river. During that time, I identified a common merganser as a kingfisher, a muskrat as an otter, and a whole, distant beach full of frolicking nude bathers as a herd of wild goats. I'm still sick about missing that one.

While glasses are my loss leader, they are by no means the only things I lose, and for all the anxiety and discomfort this particular enervation has caused, I do find solace in the knowledge I am not alone. Someone out there has an even worse

time with pocket knives, wrist watches, and goose calls, for the last time I checked, I had collected a half dozen of each, found in various stages of deterioration in four different corners of the state. I have also picked up fly boxes, canteens, life vests, and one very old, very rusty .44 caliber buffalo revolver with an octagonal barrel that was lying on a flat rock near a cave above the Palouse River. It was a perfect place to sit and tie your boots, and I'd give anything to know who left it there and whether his wife, too, rolled her eyes and said, "What's new?" when he told her it was missing.

The fact is, sportsmen and women have made a veritable swap meet of the outdoors. For every item I misplace while fishing, hunting, or camping, I find another. As Lacey is quick to point out, there is seldom equity between what I lose and what I find, but a guy's got to take things as they come. So what if the glasses I lost were worth $237 and the pocket knife I found a mere $5.95? Whoever picked up the glasses didn't get such a good deal either, unless he happened to be 20–40 in one eye and 20–200 in the other with a severe astigmatism. And who can say I didn't get the best deal last year when I "traded" a box of expensive steelhead flies for a beaten up old Tadpolly? I hadn't caught a thing with the flies, but the following week I nailed a 32–pound chinook with the plug. Best of all, the swap was made with no haggling and I didn't have to follow Lacey around to every garage sale in town.

Al Rettmann, a fishing friend of mine, recently received a letter and a stack of photos from a brother who had completed a successful whitetail hunt in eastern Texas. Though grateful for the opportunity to take a fine buck, the brother bemoaned his misfortune in losing a pair of expensive binoculars along the way. When Al shared the pictures with me, one showed the brother with his animal on the fringes of a stand of live oak. Hanging from a limb at eye level were the binoculars. I say they're not lost anymore because someone knows where they are, but Al's brother didn't see it that way when we called to tell him. He *was* gracious, though. Said he hopes someone swaps for them before they rust.

'Cause I'm not a pretty man

I imagine I'm being unreasonable, but I do not wear hunting clothes purchased through mail–order catalogues. Though the quality of most such merchandise appears to be excellent, tradition and economics dictate that neither I nor any of my gunning cronies will wear a garment that has not been rescued at least once from the Goodwill bag or the garbage. My cousin, in fact, has a brown wool cap with ear flaps, circa 1932, which has been salvaged so many times from the trash barrel it will smell forever of orange peelings and cabbage. It has captured and held a record of sorts by also being reclaimed twice from the rag bag, once from the incinerator, and once from the dog pound where it was about to be destroyed for running deer.

It hurts to admit, but there is another reason I don't buy hunting apparel from outdoor catalogues: I'm not a pretty man. Mom always thought I was kind of cute, but as I got my teeth, the cuteness wore off. Today, my eyes are deep–set, my nostrils flare, and what used to be a mere bald spot is now a barren acre. When I squint, creases in my forehead sneak down and form bags under my eyes, and when I smile, you'll see chipped front teeth and a head full of fillings. My physique, alas, has begun a southern migration, destination unknown; I have been known to clear beaches and make small children cry just by removing my shirt—not a pretty man at all.

There is no way I'm going to buy clothing from an outdoor catalogue that uses male models with bodies like Arnold Swartzenegger's and faces like Robert Redford's. I derive enough humility during the normal course of a hunting season, and I don't need to feel inadequate by comparison in a bush shirt, a tweed shooting jacket, or a pair of long underwear.

And speaking of long underwear, I find the catalogue ads for these garments particularly abasing. I always assumed longjohns were intentionally cut big for comfort. When I slip into a pair there is ample room in the crotch to store a sack lunch or a limit of quail. Where do advertisers in outdoor catalogues find male models who not only *fill* their underwear but make it look snug? I could never trust the endorsement of anyone who can wear his thermals snug without quail in them.

I am much more inclined to show interest in a product worn by an individual who at least *seems* to be actively participating in the sport for which he is modeling merchandise. Not only are they too pretty, the men in the catalogues who are supposed to be hunting game do nothing in the pictures but stand around staring into the distance with their rifles over one shoulder. This seems particularly ridiculous when they are wearing only

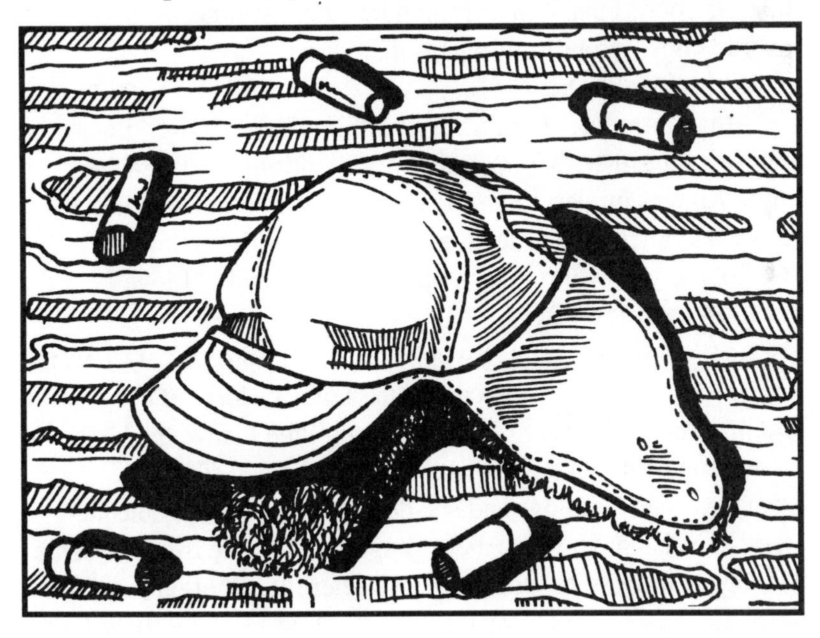

long underwear; it makes you wonder what they are looking for. I know *I* wouldn't hang around the 'ol hunting camp very long with guys like that. Evidently, these fellows don't stalk alder thickets for bear, they don't agonize through marshland for grouse, and they are never in the presence of blood or grime. I would feel a lot more confident about their products if they were crawling, crouching, sweating, or swatting mosquitoes. They need to get dirty and excited and be human.

Before our anniversary last year, my wife got her hands on an outdoor mail–order catalogue, and when we exchanged gifts I became the owner of a ragg wool wingshooting sweater with brushed leather shoulder and elbow patches.

"What is this?" I asked, turning it over in my hands.

"It's a blend of 75% wool and 25% nylon," she said, "and it's guaranteed to look good on any hunting trip."

"And that's it?"

"The catalogue said it was durable and would keep you warm, and oh my, but you should have seen the fellow modeling it!"

"My Army surplus parka keeps me warm," I said grumpily. "I've been wearing it ten years with no problems, and as for looking good, I can't even remember the last time we had a fashion show in our hunting camp."

"I can take it back."

Almost too late, I realized what I had been doing. Lacey had given a gift with love and good intentions, and now her lower lip was quivering and I was recalling some advice my father had once given me about wives and quivery lower lips. "Of course you won't take it back, dear," I said. "I love it. I'll bet it will last forever."

As it turns out, the ragg wool sweater will probably last even longer, for in the unorganized darkness of my closet, it hangs with less than an hour's wear. I put it on each time I leave the house to go hunting, and I take it off when I get to the car. The little woman will never know, and she deserves that type of consideration; she also ordered me a 20–gauge side by side from the same catalogue, and I've never swung a sweeter little shotgun.

It's stinkweed to me

After more than three decades of tramping around the diverse habitats of this great country, I figured I could pretty much identify every wild flower, bush, tree, or weed that grew here. Flowers, of course, had blossoms. Most of these were yellow or white, though blue and pink were popular colors also. You hardly ever saw a gray one. Bushes were taller than flowers but not as tall as trees, and weeds were what grew in my lawn. It was all pretty simple, and though Lacey coerced me into "broadening my horizons" by enrolling in a plant identification class through the local community college, I managed, nevertheless, to keep learning to a minimum.

"It's called *Wild Flora of the West*," she told me. "It runs for two days and we can get college credit if we want."

"I knew a wild Flora once," I said absently. "Of course, she wasn't as wild as wild Ginger, but once a car load of us went to Hailey's Pond to do some skinny dippin' and. . . ."

"Spare me," Lacey interrupted, and I was fairly certain it was more an edict than a request. "Are we going, or would you rather stay home with Margaret's kids? I told her we'd babysit if we weren't doing anything."

"Jake the Snake and Emily the Swamp Woman?" I whined. "What kind of option is that? Kids that age need to stay with their mothers. At home. In a playpen with bars and a security lock."

"Come on," Lacey said. "They're not all bad. So they like to pet your mounted birds. All kids like to touch soft things."

"That's true," I conceded, "but all kids do not like to stack soft things one on top of another and then coat them with peanut butter and jam."

"Shall we take the class, then?" Lacey asked sweetly.

"You talked me into it," I said.

The following day, Lacey and I met our instructor and 20 classmates near a bicycle trail on the edge of town. Each of us was given a plant taxonomy book, a hand lens, and a dissecting kit, and almost immediately, we were peering down at a flat–topped plant bearing numerous white flowers in small heads clustered at about the same level.

"It's stinkweed," I said, bending down to pinch a pungent flower from the stem. "We used to chase the girls with 'em when I was a kid and rub 'em on the backs of their necks." I straightened up just in time to be hit full in the face with one of Lacey's patented glares.

"He had a very boring childhood," she apologized to the instructor and the other curious eyes, "but he's still prone to fits of nostalgia."

The instructor pulled his glasses down on his nose and studied me over the top of the wire frames. Then he cleared his throat with a rather dramatic "Hu–rumph" and tugged at his moustache. "It's actually a yarrow," he said. "Achilles lanulosa of the family Compositae. Also called milfoil or tansy. Yarrow could be confused with dusty maidens or dogfennels, but. . . ."

"What's this one here with the purple flowers right next to the stinkweed?" I asked, hunkering beside it.

The instructor was frozen in mid–sentence with his mouth open. He closed it when I smiled, but appeared to be sizing me up. "Hairy vetch," he said without expression.

"Same to ya, fella," I said, rising.

"Not *wretch,* dear," Lacey said, jumping between us. "The nice man said *vetch.* V–E–T–C–H. It's the name of the plant." The instructor smiled nervously and turned back to the other students and Lacey planted one of her sharpened elbows hard, just under my rib cage.

"This next plant," the instructor said as I gasped for breath, "is called a meadow salsify. The meadow salsify has a white, milky substance once used by native Americans as a numbing agent. The roots taste very much like oysters and. . . ."

"Milkweed," I gasped. "We always called it milkweed. Eddie Shawgo and I used to chase the girls with it and. . . ."

Lacey had hold of my elbow and was ushering me toward the car through a patch of silky–leafed plants about six inches in height. "Bombastic nitwit!" she hissed.

"Looks more like bunny ears," I said. "Jim Farrow and I used to chase the girls with it and when we'd catch 'em. . . ."

"Yeah, yeah," Lacey sighed tightening her grip. "I know. I know. When you'd catch 'em, they'd have to marry you." She sighed deeply. "And I never was very fast."

The enlightenment of Enos

When I was still in high school, I inherited a suspicious looking setter from an uncle on his way to southeast Asia. For many years, I had coveted such a four–legged hunting companion, but it didn't take many trips afield with Zackery to realize that comparing him to a bird dog was like looking for similarities in a hobby horse and a Tennessee Walker. In addition to his apparent lack of gray matter, Zackery possessed the olfactory discrimination of a zucchini and the charm of a canker sore. When Mrs. Goldburg down the street angrily deposited a box of Zack's progeny on our back porch, my mother gave him and 80 pounds of kibble to the carpet cleaner.

In retrospect, Zack didn't get a fair shake. With poor breeding, zero training, and no chance to bond, he had little if any chance for the mediocrity I demanded. The only thing Zack did well was run, and because I felt the same about dog kennels as I did about goldfish bowls, that's what he did. His unrestrained, whirlwind dashes about the neighborhood were fun for him but a problem for neighbors who had set their garbage cans out, put pies on the back porch to cool, or left their tennis shoes on the patio.

In the years since Zack, I have owned a number of good bird dogs, and I now know the nicest thing an owner can do for a canine partner is keep him penned. A penned dog does not get worms eating the neighbor's garbage, he does not play "chicken" with cars or trains, and he does not enter into hasty and sometimes embarrassing relationships with a flashy bitch from the other side of the tracks. Several months ago, I shared this philosophy with a neighbor, Enos Groom, but it was not until just recently that Enos started keeping his big shorthair, Jobe, in a kennel.

If the truth be known, I had absolutely nothing to do with Enos's enlightenment. The credit belongs to another neighbor, Sam Suppola, who lives across the way. Sam and Enos had not been on speaking terms since the day Jobe knocked Sam from his bicycle, but in fairness to Jobe, it must be said the incident was not malicious and he was far more interested in catching Mrs. Shuck's cat than wreaking havoc on Sam. Nevertheless, my neighbor lost a sizable hunk from his left calf when the bike crashed in the gravel. Sam says he could have forgiven that particular trespass, but what he couldn't forgive was the fact Jobe then returned, sniffed around a bit, and *ate* the missing piece of flesh. After that, Sam says, the dog thought they were related and began inviting himself over to peruse the contents of his garbage cans, to supervise his barbecues, and to make brown spots on his shrubs.

Sam tried to discourage Jobe's "neighborly" behavior by yelling, but usually Jobe would hesitate only until Sam was hoarse. Sam then bought an air rifle but didn't have the heart to use it, so he resorted to hurling sticks and pine cones which Jobe just retrieved and chewed to shreds on the lawn. Jobe thought it great fun, and when Sam couldn't find a missile in his own yard, Jobe would bring his own, drop it at Sam's feet, and stand back, tongue lolling, waiting to begin the game.

Finally, Sam decided nothing would be accomplished unless he appealed directly to Jobe's master, but though Enos always made a token effort to keep his dog at home for several days after such protests, he insisted Jobe was a house dog and refused to build a kennel. Pretty soon, Jobe was across the street again sleeping in the flower bed or committing other doggy indiscretions in the yard. The problem evolved into a bit of a feud with Sam shoveling up the day's accumulation of bones, stool, and assorted garbage and depositing them nightly on Enos's sidewalk, and Enos angrily returning them the next morning.

Eventually, the problem was solved through psychological conditioning. Sam purchased a whole octopus at the fish market and staked it out in his back yard, After it lay several days in the sun, Jobe found it, and being a dog, began to roll, delighting in accumulating as much fishy stench as possible. Then, he trotted proudly home to share his nefarious aroma with the Groom family. This went on for days. Bath followed bath, but afterwards, Jobe would immediately refamiliarize himself with the octopus. When their house and clothing began to retain the distinctive, putrid aroma of decaying fish, Enos gave in, leveled the raspberry patch, and built a kennel. He said he'd been planning on doing it for a long time. Sam said he doubted that, but he was pleased anyway. He also wondered what he would do with the cow stomachs he had ordered in case the octopus didn't work.

The Lincoln Log syndrome

His feet planted solidly apart, knees bent slightly, the man brandishes the chain saw like an assault rifle. Through oily, acrid smoke, sweat glistens on his bulging biceps and naked chest, and above the taut, fine line of his mouth, a scarred hardhat is pushed back to expose a curly hank of virile, dark hair.

The chain saw roars, chewing at the huge pine and spitting its white flesh contemptuously to the ground; the tree shudders as the undercut is completed. The long, dentate blade withdraws, growling impatiently, then bites again into the soft trunk—this time from the opposite side. In seconds the vanquished giant bows, leans forward, and submits. Living fiber cracks and tears as the tree plummets downward amid ripping branches and a lusty, victorious "Tim–m–m–ber–r–r!"

The conquest complete, the man steps back from the stump and spits. Then he spits again. He has watched macho men on the TV sports network. He knows macho men spit a lot. He revs the saw and wades into the sea of fallen branches and needles, spitting and severing limbs. The limbs are not his own.

This is how I thought it would be when I first dreamed of building a log house. Strong, determined, virile, and a good spitter, I, like my forefathers who wielded crosscut saws and axes, would conquer and reduce to possession an American wilderness—in this case a 20–acre woodlot north of town surrounded by apartment complexes and owned by my wife's mother.

"You want to *what*?" Lacey was folding laundry, hurriedly separating my shorts from the dish towels. She was convinced the prolonged union of the two would result in bizarre and mind–altering rituals that would provide steamy headlines for the tabloids.

"I want to build a log house," I told her again. "From scratch."

Lacey grunted, smiled absently, and jerked another dish towel from the gaping maw of my boxers. Then she plunged both hands into the laundry basket and came up with a squirming mass of cotton and elastic. She began to hum the theme song to Davey Crockett.

"Lacey," I said, pushing aside the laundry basket, "you're not listening. I want to build a log house; I've always wanted to build a log house. Now that your mother is talking about thinning that 20 acres, I think we should act on our fantasy. I think. . . ."

"Fold," Lacey said, pushing a pile of pillow cases toward me. She glared, but a smile kept twitching the corners of her mouth. "And what do you mean *"our"* fantasy? *My* fantasy leans more toward warm sand and coconut suntan oil."

"Okay, okay," I conceded. *"My* fantasy." Then I related to her the image of the man of my dreams—the man I could be. I left out nothing. Lacey listened with only a few mirthful snorts.

"But you don't have a hardhat or a chain saw. You don't have bulging muscles or dark hair, either. In fact, you don't have *any* hair," she said, proving once again she has absolutely no imagination, is incapable of a good fantasy, and has a mean streak besides.

Despite my wife's frivolous comments, I was determined to pursue my dream, and when I began drawing up house plans and calculating the number of logs I would need, she waded into the muddied waters. Lacey said it was because turning me loose alone in the woods with a chain saw was a threat to our relations with neighboring Canada and perhaps even world peace, but I knew the real reason: Lacey had seen the bay window I had included in the floorplan, and there isn't a woman alive who doesn't want a house with a bay window. There isn't a man alive who knows why women want that bay window, either, but I personally suspect that some sort of weird but pleasurable rite is performed there just prior to their Wednesday afternoon bowling league.

The next morning, Lacey and I loaded the truck with an assortment of begged and borrowed logging apparati, some of which we didn't recognize. Our primary benefactor was Durwood Pickle, our magnanimous but somewhat eccentric neighbor. If Durwood was a pair of pants, he'd be "slightly irregular." He had already donated a chain saw, a hardhat, and two pairs of fuzzy slippers to our endeavor, but as we pulled out of the driveway, he hailed us and came across the yard dragging a long–handled device with a pointed metal tip and a single tong like an ice hook.

"You gonna take a peavey?" he asked when Lacey rolled down the window.

Lacey fixed Durwood with a glare that should have melted his polyester bell bottoms. "If it's any of your business, Durwood," she said, "I already went." When we turned the corner, Durwood was still frozen, open–mouthed, on his front lawn, holding his peavey and trying to figure out what had transpired.

Actually, Lacey and I had hoped to cut more than a single log that first day, but as events developed, we felt pretty good to get just one. In fact, when it finally smashed to the ground, narrowly missing the cab of my pickup, I was almost giddy. There was a whole lot more to downing a pine than making an undercut and yelling "*Tim–m–m—ber–r–r–r*!"

The worst mistake we made was assuming the tree could be made to fall where we wanted it to fall despite its slight lean in the opposite direction. When, instead of crashing downward, it twisted on its stump, remained upright, and pinned Durwood's $400 chain saw beneath 2,000 pounds of trunk, I was extremely disappointed. Durwood, as I mentioned, was a little strange, and I didn't know how he would react if I told him I had abandoned his saw in the woods. It would be difficult to explain that his Stihl was hanging by the blade from a ponderosa pine somewhere on my mother–in–law's 20 acres.

Had Lacey not included in our gear as an afterthought her great–grandfather's old chicken–butchering hatchet, I'm sure our relationship with Durwood would have been tested. Even so, were I ever to encounter a similar situation, I would take my chances, because I would never, ever again try to chop down a 50–foot tree with the logging equivalent of a butter knife. When the tree finally fell four hours later, the stump looked like it had been gnawed by an intoxicated beaver with a severe underbite, my hands looked like chopped liver, and the saw bar was bent in the shape of a sickle. I didn't figure Durwood would be too happy about that, either, but getting that first log on the ground *was* a small victory for the good guys. Lacey said that towards the end of the ordeal I was whimpering. I hated to think about that, but I figured I would have numerous other weekends to fulfill my logging fantasies. My only actual disappointment was that in the excitement I had yelled "Holy Bleep!" instead of "Timber!" when the tree came down, and that dehydration had prevented me from generating enough saliva to spit.

During the following weekends, Lacey and I learned a lot about felling trees. We learned that even when they don't lean, trees do not often fall where you want them to. This point was emphasized when a large pine caught the tool box *and* the gas can, driving the can into the ground and flipping the box through the air like a comet, spewing its contents like so many asteroids. This wrong–way tendency causes the cutter to scream, but as in my first experience, it is usually something other than the traditional, macho "Tim–m–m–ber–r–r!" "Run for your life!" was one of my favorites.

We also learned that a well–sharpened chain saw is unselective, unforgiving, and always hungry. It will easily slice through boot leather and denim, but barbed wire and rocks take longer, and a purple stocking cap will bind up the teeth and kill the engine. Afterwards, this same cap won't keep your ears warm and makes you look like you're wearing a plate of purple spaghetti.

Until I began logging, I thought widow–makers were small boats. In the woods, however, a widow–maker is either a rotten limb high overhead or a tree that hangs up on another tree as it falls. You can't ignore it, and the process of bringing it to ground is every bit as terrifying as a tax audit. The first time Lacey and I experienced this aberration, I flipped a coin to determine who would mince in under the half–fallen tree and cut the other one that was holding it up. Lacey lost but refused to go. "It's called a *widow*–maker," she said. "That means *you* go."

With Lacey watching the tottering tree and me watching her for the signal to run, I went to work with the saw. Surely, I thought, this will be my opportunity to display a taut, fine–lined mouth and perhaps a little virility besides. At the very least, I figured, I can spit a couple times. Sadly, it was not to be.

Bringing down a widow–maker was terrifying, and my cotton mouth made spitting impossible. The word "trust" took on a new meaning as I wielded the saw blindly while watching Lacey's face for the slightest twitch that might indicate a change in the tree's position. Midway through the ordeal, I stopped cutting long enough to remind her I had recently buried a large sum of money, and were I to die unexpectedly, she wouldn't find it in a million years.

Eventually, the widow–maker came down—the first of several to so enchant me during the next several weeks. After the fifth or sixth experience, I was compromising some of my visions of becoming a man's man and concentrating heavily on maintaining a few masculine characteristics. Even this modest goal, however, was challenged one Saturday when I held the upturned chain saw in my lap while attempting to make a repair. Before long, a burning sensation in my groin area suggested all was not well. Dripping fuel from the saw's gas tank had saturated my pants and underwear, creating a considerable amount of heat on my most tender parts.

Reacting quickly if not rationally, I took off in the direction of the pickup, yowling like a tomcat in love as I tried to shed my clothes. Succeeding only in getting my jeans and shorts to my ankles where they were intercepted by my boots, I nevertheless continued a mad, yowling hop around the truck until I stumbled and fell backwards. Seizing this opportunity, Lacey jumped on my chest and attempted to douse the burning with a can of diet root beer. In the meantime, her mother, who had just driven up to see how we were doing, jumped to some erroneous but understandable conclusions. We didn't even know she was in the vicinity until we heard her unbelieving, "Oh my gawd!"

An hour or so later, the fire between my legs had cooled somewhat, Lacey's shaken mother had returned to town, and I felled the last tree of the day. When it dropped, its branches caught the tip of another, smaller tree, bending it to the ground at a right angle and pinning it there like a catapult. When I waded into the foliage and began limbing the larger tree, I inadvertently straddled this catapult, and when my saw released the tension by cutting through the pinning branch, the smaller tree whipped upright with a whuppp!

Lacey later told her friends I was flung into oblivion, but

that is entirely inaccurate as I flew scarcely more than six feet. Lacey also told her friends I invented several new words, but that is wrong, also; I had known them for a long time. It was just that I was saving them for a special occasion, and nothing is quite so special to a man as being racked in the groin by a catapulting yellow pine. It beats fingernail smashing and shin scraping by a mile.

Lacey wanted to laugh, but there was something about my face that made her think better; there was always the chance I would renege on my promise to build her a bay window. "Well, Mr. Davy Crockett," she said when my eyes began to uncross, "that will make the highlight films for sure."

Cautiously, I rocked up to a sitting position. "Did we bring the peavey?" I croaked.

"Right here," Lacey said. She looked at me incredulously. "You're not going back to work are you?"

My tongue worked slowly across my lips, pushing aside fragments of spider webs and forest floor. "Roll me to the truck, dear," I said. "I'm going home." Then, almost as an afterthought, I tried to spit, but the saliva caught the end of my graying mustache and hung there like a Christmas ornament on a frosted tree. I grinned feebly at my wife. "Just checking," I said. Obviously, the man of my dreams was still just the man of my dreams.

By the lunches he keeps

A friend, Bob Aho, makes dog houses for a living, a rather seasonal and financially precarious occupation. Bob used to be a high school educator with a guaranteed income, medical benefits, and a three–month summer vacation, and I'm not sure whether the vocational change says more about Bob or teaching. I do know, however, that he is a great guy to have along on a fishing or hunting trip because he knows how to pack a lunch.

You can tell a lot about a man by the lunches he puts together. Bob's, for example, reflect his philosophy that we only go around once and if we do it right, that's all we need. His lunches are unusual enough to astound, nutritious enough to sustain without being stuffy, and most importantly, big enough to share. His cooler always contains just the right proportions of gooey candy bars to crisp apples or carrot sticks, baloney sandwiches to barbecued halibut fillets, and bottled, home–made fruit juice to caffeine–rich soft drinks. For dessert, choose from fresh chocolate chip cookies, imported English eclairs, or G.I. pound cake in a squatty, Army–green can. Bob Aho, like the rest of the men I hunt and fish with, expects to get dirty and wet and tired in the course of a day afield. He sweats, falls down, and wears the same worn pants through all seasons. When it comes to lunch, however, Bob has class, and his lunches are civilized.

I used to say a man could tell if his wife loved him by whether or not she put lettuce on his sandwiches. Later, I decided plain liverwurst was a fair indicator of love as long as the little woman didn't complain too much as she made them. Lately, though, I've been making my own sandwiches and feeling fortunate to have finished my laundry in time to get in a few hours afield. I seldom use lettuce, and I think there's a message for me there somewhere, but I don't care to dwell on it.

Actually, there is a lot more than philosophical insights to be learned by studying a man's lunches. When my friend, Herb Ladding, shows up with only a loaf of bread and a gnawed turkey carcass, I know Herb has been out late the night before. I used to do the same thing until they started making alcohol more potent and nights a lot shorter. Somehow, when the head throbs, the eyes bulge, the stomach is dancing the funky chicken, and the mouth is filled with cotton, making sandwiches is not an early morning priority. Getting the cap off a bottle of aspirin is a lot more important. "Day After" lunches are not necessarily inadequate, but they always take up more room than others because they consist of a few bulky items that can be thrown into a cooler with minimal movement. It is not uncommon to find whole hams and sacks of oranges as "Day After" lunches.

"The Alarm Didn't Go Off" lunches are similar to "Day After" lunches but have more variety because movements are not restricted by a hangover. Characteristically, an "Alarm Didn't" hunter or fisherman will tear about the kitchen throwing whatever he sees into a large plastic garbage bag. My brother–in–law, Thayer, once piled into the car on a duck–gunning trip with a half case of vanilla pudding, an unopened package of napkins, two bars of soap, a box of Cocoa Puffs, and an assortment of jars containing pickles, green olives, and maraschino cherries. He didn't bring a fork or spoon.

"Company's In Town" lunches are a gastronomical phenomenon. My friend, Eddie, says he can't wait until his folks visit each year. To be sure, his lunches improve dramatically when they do. Eddie is one of those rare individuals whose wife still gets up, however begrudgingly, to pack his fishing lunch, but increasingly skimpy sandwiches and black bananas reflect the fact the honeymoon ended some time ago. When his parents are staying over, however, his lunch sack bulges with a copious variety of carefully–prepared and wrapped goodies put together the night before as his cheerful, loving bride visits in the kitchen with her mother–in–law. For the past seven years, Eddie has been trying to get his folks to rent the room in the basement during the steelhead season.

Personally, I think my own repasts in the field are better than most. Because I don't function well before mid–morning, I usually make my lunch the night before. Then, I leave it in the refrigerator when I walk out the door at five a.m. Around noon, my pathetic whimperings and growling stomach always persuade buddies to share. This insures variety and saves me the expense of buying my meal in a small–town cafe or resort diner. The only problem is that by late afternoon *everyone* is hungry due to reduced rations, and I am obligated to purchase hamburgers, fries, and milkshakes for the whole group on the way home. My wife says there is also a message there, but I don't care to dwell on that one, either.

Second chance

Sometime during the long summer of my childhood, my father took me aside for a serious discussion. "Fix what you can," he told me, "and live with what you can't." The occasion, as I remember it, was my first attempt to clean some doggy residue from my sneakers.

A week after I returned from my first trip to the Alaska Peninsula, I was trying to recall my father's sage advice as I moped about the house, mourning my disappointing "hunt of a lifetime." Not only had bad weather and mechanical problems cut my trip short, I had sadly misjudged the size of what I thought was a trophy caribou. Then, the pictures came back from the developer, and my wife, Lacey, liked what she saw. "I think you should do it again," she said, "and take me, too." That evening, she cut a slit in the top of a large juice can and started another "Alaska Fund" with five dollars from the grocery budget. From my standpoint, taking a non–hunting wife on a caribou hunt wasn't an ideal arrangement, but it was certainly better than not going at all.

After an agonizing three–year wait, we were finally on a floatplane drifting through Clark Pass on our way to a familiar little lake on the Alaska Peninsula. Then, the plane was touching down and gliding across the water, the pontoons scraping gravel on the lake bed. When we stopped, the pilot was out the door in an instant, obviously anxious to get us unloaded. He looked up into a darkening sky. "The weather's got me worried," he said. "There's a front moving in. If I can get you two set up quickly, I can beat it home."

A scant two hours later, Lacey and I lay on our backs encased in rip–stop nylon, transmogrified into a cocoon by a tent that was pushed down over our faces by gale–force winds. Only the weight of our bodies kept us from being swept away in the same direction as our paper towels, our coffee filters, and the cooking fly.

"Well, isn't this great!" I growled. "A repeat of the last time, only earlier. Three thousand miles, three thousand dollars, and now this. The next thing I know, the earth will open up and. . . ."

"Alan," Lacey interrupted, her mouth but inches from the nylon above her, "are we in a life–threatening situation?"

The wind howled, the rain beat against us, and fingers of cold air probed my underside, but suddenly, something had changed. Perhaps we *were* in a life–threatening situation, but the innocence and calmness of my wife's question made me smile. She was giving me something—the opportunity to play the protector, and I was grateful. "If you forgot your reading material," I told her, "you're liable to be bored to death. Other than that, though, we'll be okay."

Lacey tried to turn her head, but in our cramped quarters, the movement pressed the tip of her nose against the tip of mine. The sensation was surprisingly pleasant, but I crossed my eyes and made a face just the same because this was a *hunting* trip, doggone it, not a second honeymoon.

"You're weird," she said.

"Thanks," I replied.

We lay silently, nose to nose for several more moments while I studied my wife's freckles. "There's eight," I said at last. "I thought there were only seven, but there's eight."

The storm raged on. Lacey and I lay in a tent that was never more than two feet high, and we did something many married couples never make time for—we talked, *and* we listened, and between the two we ate some toothpaste together because it was all we could reach. During the third hour we covered more serious topics like childhood phobias, first dates, and the horrors of adolescent love. Later, we made a list of the ten most worthless classes ever offered in college, discussed politics, doctors, lawyers, and food, and went on to analyze personalities, motivations, and words we couldn't spell. I was disappointed when we both fell asleep before I'd had a chance to talk about the dream where my teeth turn to sand.

Thirty–six hours later, our second dawn brought uninhibited

sunlight, and the world outside our tent, though battered, was friendly again. Lacey picked blueberries and created magnificent, purple pancakes while I searched for firewood. That day, we scouted caribou, appraised their velveted racks, and caught grayling from the outlet stream. We photographed clouds and ptarmigan and red fox, and in the settling light of evening, poked at the campfire and talked quietly and wished we could stay where we were and be what we had become forever. On the fourth day, we crawled to within 50 feet of a pair of sparring bull caribou, and I shot the trophy I had long dreamed of.

On day five,we slept in, puttered around the campfire with our coffee, and then caped the bull. Next, we stripped the velvet, a tedious, time–consuming affair that took most of the rest of the day and broke the three fingernails Lacey had salvaged from the caping and boning operations. That evening, I attended her cut, chapped hands and she tried to rub a persistent spasm from my lower back, and despite our weariness, we sat up late outside the tent holding hands like a couple silly kids, watching the late–setting sun slice our lake into two perfect, golden halves.

The plane was there on the sixth day—too soon, I thought, as we had been wishing for something to prolong our stay. "Guess it was quite a storm you had out here," our plot said cautiously. "I imagine there was some down time. You two still married?" He didn't laugh.

"Even better than that," I grinned. "But I never did get to talk about the way my teeth turn to sand in the middle of the night."

"Or why my speech teacher wore his toupee backwards," Lacey giggled. My wife's hair had lost the last of its curl and smelled of wood smoke, her shirt was rumpled and blood-stained, and she wore no makeup as she stuffed dirtier clothes in a purple duffel; I'd never seen her lovelier.

Dear Uncle Al:

Thought you would want to know—Lacey found your glass eye at the bottom of my decoy bag. I must say it gave her a start. I'm always telling folks around Loon Lake that my wife has a lot of kid in her, but if I hadn't seen it myself, I would have never believed she could yell that loud, jump that high, or run that fast. The Reverand Mr. Sinn, who was at the front door when she came around the side of the house, couldn't believe it either. Lacey and I played on the church softball team a few years back, and Rev. Sinn always said that between home and first, Lacey was slower than the Second Coming. Just goes to show what a little motivation can do.

Anyway, Uncle, your eye is in the mail. Too bad you already bought a new one, but I imagine it won't hurt to keep a spare as you seem to have a proclivity for losing the thing. Was it last year or the year before that you took it out to show Brian Hess and then left it sitting on your empty plate at the Loon Lake Cafe? They're still talking about that one. Evelyn Longmeir, the waitress, didn't even know it was there until the fry cook went out the back door without opening the screen.

The next time we go hunting, Uncle, it would probably be a good idea to keep your glass eye in place, though I must admit it was a pretty good joke. The look on Mike's face when he saw it sitting there on the bench next to him was probably worth the inconvenience and expense. I guess we'll never know how it got into the decoy bag, but I think it probably happened when that flock of widgeons swooped by the set and we went through our Three Stooges drill trying to metamorphose from comedians to duck hunters before they made another pass.

For some reason, Loon Lake seems different this year. I can't quite put my finger on it—an unnatural tenseness rather than anything I can see. The same old faces are still at the post office, the feed store is still offering six months worth of free round worm medicine to whoever correctly guesses the weight of the summer's biggest lake trout, and Tilly Shuck is again preparing to resell a year's worth of borrowed tools at her annual yard sale. (Lacey says if I get there early this year, I can probably pick up our snow shovel and wheelbarrow for next to nothing). A typical summer around here passes like a leaf on a brook. Sometimes the days get caught in the backwater and swirl lazily around going nowhere. Those are my favorite. Then, they'll find an eddy and drift off again, but always slowly and without much intensity, except you know there's something to look forward to—a family reunion in Morgan Park or the Loon Society's annual convention and car wash. I like those, too, as long as there's plenty of fishing time between. But this summer. . .this summer seems jerky, like someone is throwing rocks in the water, and you never know when you'll get wet or be pushed out into the current. Lacey says it's because of Sammy.

You haven't met Sammy, have you? She's Morry Francik's vizsla/setter/rocket. Morry had been having marital difficulties again and was living in a camp trailer on a rented lot in town. I told him I'd keep Sammy until he got back together with his wife, but now I'm beginning to think Morry is willing to sacrifice the marriage to get rid of the dog. The problem is, Sammy is three years old, a pretty little thing with after–burners and nary a lick of obedience training. She can run the hundred in a blink, has a vertical leap of eight feet, and chases anything that flies, including bees, robins, and the shadows of airplanes. In the kennel, she is a picky eater, but outside has shown a preference for sun screen, air mattresses, and inner tubes. You can imagine how much fun she is on the beach. I let her out of the kennel this morning at 7:00 and she disappeared heading north. At 7:04, she reappeared from the south under a full head of steam. I'm certain that in those four minutes she circumnavigated the globe. It's no fun having a dog like that around, Uncle Al; she makes me nervous, and I don't think she particularly appreciates my company anyway. Any suggestions?

The wild game dinner wasn't the same without you this year. Some say it was better, but personally, I missed your goose pepperoni. I did have the opportunity to try roast beaver for the first time, however—something I'd wanted to do since reading those mountain men tales as a kid. I must say that roast beaver considerably lowered my esteem for mountain men. There were 50 people here this year, and they were almost exactly split between those who "wouldn't try beaver in a million years" and those who tried it but wouldn't try it *again* in a million years.

Are you coming up in October? There's a little old lady down the road who owns ten acres of marsh off the lake. She says we can hunt mallards there if we promise to pluck one for her now and then. She's really sweet but kind of deaf, and for some reason has decided my name is Howard. I've tried to tell her I'm not Howard, but I've about given up. Maybe she thinks I'm a relative or something. Maybe she wouldn't give us permission to hunt if she knew my name was Alan. It's a great spot, Uncle Al. Bring lots of shells.

Howard

Mr. Banana Head

In the 1800's, an English poet by the name of Lord Alfred Tennyson told us that in the spring, a young man's fancy turns to love. He said nothing, however, about young women having similar hormonal disruptions during that same season, an omission that has disappointed members of the male persuasion for generations. The fact is, in April and May, a woman's fancy is turned toward a general and unreasonable need to vacuum, polish, and disinfect in the name of "spring house cleaning." And, it is interesting to note that this annual cleaning frenzy is a misnomer, for it is not by any means limited to the place of abode.

My wife, Lacey, not one to shirk feminine responsibilities like shopping, worrying about her weight, and assuming immediate liability for every stray dog that walks through the yard, is also a crafty technician when it comes to delegating spring cleaning responsibilities. This means that when the big day is announced (possibly dictated by the depth of dust on the mounted dove in the dining room), the kids swab out their rooms, the garage, and the shed, and I am assigned all windows, the carpets, the upstairs closets, any shelf higher than six feet, the boat, my den, and the basement. It is also strongly suggested each spring that I clean my truck, but I always conveniently forget my promise to "think about it" because it is, after all, MY truck, a vehicle Lacey barely knows and never rides in. It is used only during outdoor recreational pursuits by myself and other similarly–inclined male persons, and when *I* think it needs cleaning, I might just do it.

The fact is, my truck is held together with grime. The mud of countless back roads has hardened to form a protective shield that prevents the fenders from falling off. The upholstery looks and smells like the piece of carpeting in the dog's house, and I don't worry about it ripping, fraying, or fading, because it already has. The spot next to me shines with a glass–like sheen, the result of many seasons of dog drool, dropped potato chips, and spilled coffee (heavy with cream and sugar). The floorboards are encrusted in candy bar wrappers, mud, gravel, banana peels, sprouting weed seeds, pop cans, feathers, and dozens of defective, yellow, stick–up notes with secret, scrawled phone numbers and directions that will take me to secret, wonderful hunting and fishing spots when I get them dried out and deciphered. Without this wondrous layer of weekend souvenirs, I would be looking through gaping, rusted holes to the road below.

My truck is like a small–town mom and pop variety store. No matter where I am, no matter what the situation, my truck will not (barring unannounced days off) let me down. Never, never, for example, will I have to worry about being caught on a bear hunt 80 miles into the mountains north of town without a #2 plastic wing nut or a 3–foot length of 3/8–inch plastic tubing, as at some juncture along the way, I tossed both of these items behind the seat. I also carry tools in the cab that will fix eye glasses, remove choke tubes, pull nails, jimmy doors, cut pipe, calculate elevation, and cauterize wounds. Somewhere under the seat are four varieties of tape, a band saw, a serrated knife, a box of plastic bags, and a curry comb. Some of this stuff just showed up.

My truck is a spare closet. It regurgitates dry socks, stocking hats, quilted wool shirts, and light gloves—but not always when I need them. I have had to use socks to keep my hands warm and a wool shirt like a scarf to cover freezing ears, but being a dog owner has given me lots of practice in the art of feeling ridiculous, and I don't mind more than a little any more.

Oft–times, these items of apparel are coughed up in combination with the previously–mentioned floorboard gunk—like the pea–green aviator's hat with woolen ear flaps crusted in forgotten, dried, banana. I wore it out of desperation on a bitter cold bird hunting trip this past year and was glad to have it. My gunning partners called me "Mr. Banana Head" and said I smelled like a fruit salad, but I thought that imminently better than "Earless Al," which is what I would have become had I faced that wind all day without a hat.

Sorry, Jeremiah

Three nights in a row I experienced the unusual dream. Three nights in a row my yellow baseball cap floated forlornly atop the polished surface of the water. It warranted an immediate analysis, but time was precious, so I filed my disturbing vision for future rumination and helped Laurence John unload his 12–foot canoe. Before me stretched the Swan Lake Canoe System—seven lakes, seven portages, and then the Moose River. According to Laurence, I could make the float in four easy days and end up at his fishing lodge where the Moose met the Kenai. It was perfect.

For years, I had fantasized about this Alaska canoeing adventure. Subsistence. Survival. A middle–aged survivor versus an unforgiving land; Jeremiah Johnson (a personal hero), Jim Bridger, and John Wayne all rolled up into one lean, self–reliant hunk of manliness. I would fish for my suppers, boil lake water to drink. So what if I had never before paddled a canoe? I'd watched old trappers do it on the "Late, Late Show" dozens of times.

After Laurence's departure back down the boggy rut that passed as a road, I slid the aluminum craft into the glassy blackness of tiny Portage Lake. The sun rested just on the horizon as I kneeled in the stern, shoved the paddle into the mud, and pushed off. Two strokes on the left; two strokes on the right. Switch and repeat. A piece of cake. Approaching the middle of the lake, I noticed that each time the paddle changed sides, it dripped water onto the gear stashed before me, so I experimented, swinging it over my shoulder and behind my head when going from port to starboard. Jeremiah, I thought, would have been proud of my ingenuity. Unfortunately, I knocked the baseball cap from my head on the fourth or fifth stroke. Twisting to retrieve it, I capsized.

I had always wondered how I would react to a life–threatening situation, and oddly enough, my first emotion was embarrassment. When I surfaced, three thoughts flashed through my mind. The initial one was, "I hope no one saw me do that." The second was, "I'll die out here if no one saw me do that," and the third, a rather feeble, "Sorry, Jeremiah."

Draping myself over the partially submerged but upright canoe, panting with fear, and suppressing a crazy desire to ask for an instant replay, I assessed the situation. Then I swore loudly for a few minutes and assessed it again. My tent was still wedged in the bow. My sleeping bag floated before me in a plastic garbage bag. To my left was the paddle, and next to that floated the yellow baseball cap; this was good. Somewhere below me in 15 feet of water were my cooking utensils, hatchet, knife, cigarettes and lighter, fishing gear, and $800 worth of photographic equipment; this wasn't good. In fact, it was downright disappointing.

Overcoming a desire to cling forever to the relative safety of my waterlogged canoe, I swam to retrieve what few items remained afloat. Next, I placed both hands on the vessel's stern and began kicking my sodden load toward shore. The moment I touched bottom, I knew I would live a while longer, but I don't recall the thought providing much immediate comfort. I was wet, I was shivering, I was without basic survival tools, and I couldn't count on anyone coming along for weeks; Laurence had said so. My best bet was to forge ahead. My "Great Adventure" had lasted two minutes. The "Great Ordeal" was just beginning.

That night I shivered naked in a damp sleeping bag, watching fingers of mist curl off the surface of Portage Lake, listening to the eerie call of the loon which ghosted in and out of view offshore. Nearby, a quartet of wolves howled an off–key medley of old meat–eater favorites, and something large and noisy crunched through the brush nearby. Moaning softly, I slithered into the bottom six inches of my sleeping bag.

At dawn, my wet clothes were spread over a stunted spruce to await the sun. By noon, everything was reasonably dry, but I was scratching mosquito bites in places no mosquito had a right to have been. Dressing quickly, I loaded my now meager possessions aboard the Devil Craft and skirted the shoreline to the first take–out. I was hungry but had no food, and thirsty but afraid to drink the water without first boiling it. With neither matches, lighter, nor kettle, however, this presented a problem. Beaver fever, a stomach and intestinal disorder caused by a parasite in lakes and rivers had, I'd been told, the capacity to consign an incautious camper to progressive stages of misery during which he first fears he will die, and then fears he won't.

In my naivete, I had assumed canoes, like other fishing vessels, were merely hunks of metal or fiberglass melded by man to fit a need. I had no idea they came to life in the process and took on a demented temperament. Too, I had never before attempted to portage (a French word for muscle spasm) and couldn't find the point of balance for carrying the metal beast down the narrow, mucky trail to the next lake. My first efforts resulted in a series of power spins during which I cleared a 12–foot–wide swath of underbrush and saplings as I careened out of control, the canoe twirling like a helicopter rotor above my head. Finally, in desperation, and feeling extremely un–Jeremiah Johnsonish, I rigged a harness with a piece of rope, set the aluminum monster on the trail, and like a tired plow horse, began dragging it to the small, unnamed pond between Portage and Birch Lakes. To my initial delight, the further I went, the easier it became. Partly, this was because my plow horse technique, though lacking finesse, was nevertheless effective in the slick mud, but mostly because there was a downhill gradient. In but a few minutes, in fact, I was sprinting madly down the trail, trying to keep from being overtaken and crushed by the large, banana–shaped hunk of malevolent metal behind me.

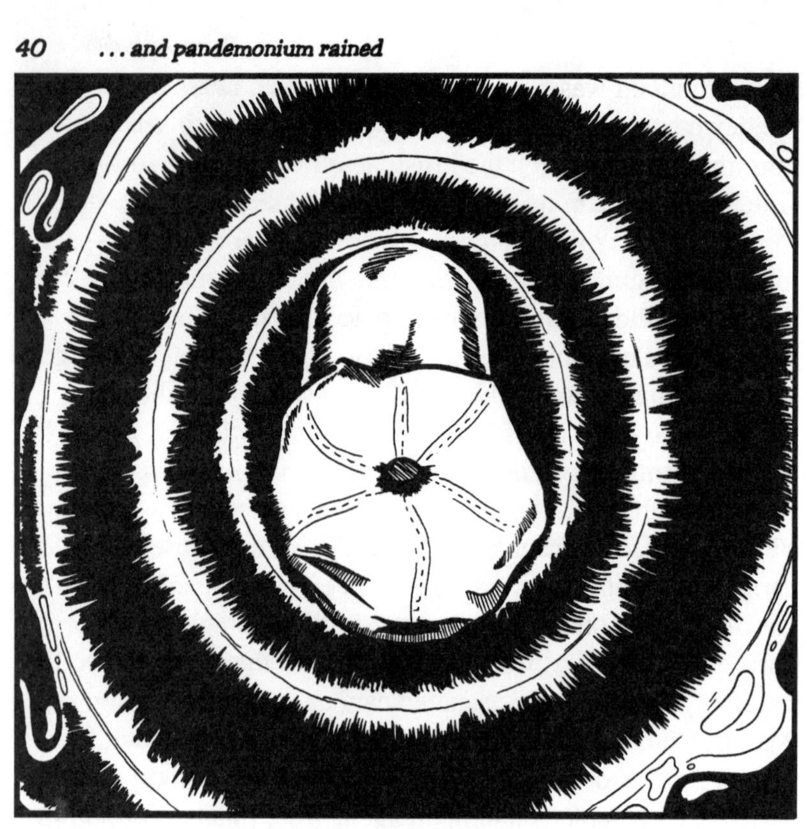

The next lake, Birch, was dimpled by rising trout, reminding me again I was hungry. I love trout, but at the time, would have eaten the dimples had I been given the opportunity. I began to fantasize about all the nourishment I had refused as a kid. What I wouldn't have given for a big plate of liver! Oh, for a bowl of broccoli or spinach! And liquids! My body was crying for liquids. How very ironic, I thought, to dehydrate surrounded by water in an area which received over 15 inches of rainfall annually. Not funny, just ironic. I took a quick slurp of lake water, hoping if I did it quickly and kept my teeth together I could filter out all the organisms waiting to cause me grief. I couldn't.

Early on day three of my ordeal, weakened by diarrhea and exertion, I was almost saved. I had completed my seventh portage, was on the Moose River, and for several hours had been attempting to navigate a canoe with an intimate attraction for rocks and overhanging vegetation. When I first heard the happy shouts, I was being swept sideways through a trough of white water, and when I miraculously floated right–side–up into the quiet pool below, there were two fishermen ahead. One had snagged a spawned–out sockeye; the other was taking pictures of the "action."

Chechakos! I thought contemptuously. No self–respecting Alaskan would be caught dead fishing for post–spawn salmon. Then, I smelled bacon cooking. Undoubtedly, there would be coffee; probably even toilet paper. Perhaps I could bum a smoke. Despite the stomach cramps, I adjusted my cap rakishly and dug the paddle into the current; I would be soft–spoken and reserved, steely–eyed and cat–like of movement. They would sense my independence and my ruggedness, feel my oneness with nature, and when we parted they would stand open–mouthed on shore, watching me maneuver my craft deftly through the tricky downstream obstacles. "Who was that guy?" one of them would ask in awe.

Slipping across the pool, I banged hard off a boulder, dropped my paddle, and capsized. Oh Lord, I thought, please don't let this be happening. Dragging myself from the shallow water, I splashed to retrieve my canoe, falling down twice and nearly losing the water–laden pants I was holding up with one hand. When I finally caught the Devil Craft, I threw myself in, disregarding the floating sleeping bag and rapidly sinking tent. I just wanted to be out of there, away from my fracturing fantasy. During the entire debacle, both fishermen stood silently, mouths open, staring. They had probably not thought to be witness to a slap–stick routine in the middle of an Alaska wilderness. "Who was that guy?" I heard one of them finally say as I hugged the bottom of my canoe and floated around a bend.

Late that night, I paddled feebly out of the Moose River and into the Kenai. Now, lights from the Great Alaska Fish Camp were winking in the half–light, and I knew Laurence would be inside working on his accounts. With one last, determined effort, I pushed the vessel toward shore—my final chance to be a mountain man. As the nose nudged the bank, I gathered all my remaining dignity and vaulted out the back—a grand move had not the water been five feet deep.

"Hey, fella," Laurence called cheerfully a few minutes later as I sloshed through the door, "you're back early!" He glanced at my dripping clothing and the puddle of water at my feet. "Didn't know it was raining," he said.

"Just started," I mumbled. My large intestine was doing a fast Texas two–step.

"You sound tired," he said. "Have a good trip?"

"Real different," I replied, eyeing the pop machine. "Real different."

Laurence shuffled some papers on his desk, yawned, and leaned back in his chair. "You know," he said, "you can be mighty proud of what you accomplished. There's not many who can say they've made a solo trip like that."

Seized by a trophy–sized cramp, I headed briskly for the bathroom, tearing at my belt. "*No one* has ever made a trip like that," I gasped. "Not even Jeremiah."

"Who?"

Without answering, I sat down and pushed the door shut with a loud slam. The gust knocked my yellow baseball cap to the waxed linoleum floor. I didn't pick it up for a long, long time.

Reason enough

A couple of Saturdays ago, some of the boys were sitting around the reloading bench in the back of Lardy James's garage when the discussion turned, as it often does, to hunting dogs. Now, all of us love our four–legged heart breakers, and none of us are afraid to stretch a tale or two about their exploits, but Enos Grooms still refused to go along with the consensus that bird dogs are capable of reason.

Tom Allen rejuvenated a dormant debate when he started talking about his Uncle Seltzer's vizsla, Goner. According to Tom, Goner plays checkers by moving the pieces with his nose, and he consistently beats Uncle Seltzer two out of three. As impressive as that was, Enos said it did nothing whatsoever to prove a dog is capable of reason. Uncle Seltzer's boy, Lam, he reminded us, can beat the old man too, and Lam is the same child who tried to unclog the toilet with a charge of black powder.

Arty Davis piped up next. Arty has a big springer named Zeus, and when it comes to getting his way in the house, Zeus is a virtuoso. Arty's wife, Marlene, is an easy touch for a shivering dog, and on a cold night, she'll not only let Zeus into the house, she'll let him crawl up on the big feather bed and sleep next to her. Now, Arty says, Zeus has learned to shiver at will, and even in August can end up in Arty's spot if he puts his mind to it.

Mike said he was sure his pointer, Katie, was capable of

reason, too, and that explained her sometimes questionable behavior afield. Katie, he says, knows if she points every bird she smells, her hunt will soon be over and she'll be back in the kennel. She therefore extends her pleasure by blinking, breaking, running amok, and disappearing for up to three hours at a time.

Once again, Enos scoffed, whereupon Arty mentioned he'd seen Enos and his dog, Jobe, go into the vet's.

"On account of his epilepsy," Enos said.

"Epilepsy?" Arty said, raising his eyebrows. "When did that start?"

Enos looked sheepish. "I got so mad at Jobe on opening day this year, I grabbed him by the collar and started dragging him to the car. Before we got there, though, he went limp. Thought I'd choked him to death," he said, wincing.

"What'd you do?" Mike asked.

"Mouth to mouth," Enos replied. "I just flopped down in the weeds and gave him mouth to mouth."

"Doesn't sound like epilepsy to me, though," Mike said. "Sounds to me like you cut off his air."

Enos hung his head. "Well, I'd hate to think I almost killed my dog," he said, "but I don't think that's the way it was. A week later we were on the way home from that wheat field up the Long Haul Road and Jobe was in the back of the station wagon. I stopped for gas at the Texaco, and when I looked back there, he had gone limp again."

"Gas fumes?" Tom asked.

"That's what I thought at first," Enos said, nodding, "so I gave him mouth to mouth and he came around again." Enos pulled nervously at his lower lip and scooted forward on his seat. "And now he's passing out real regular–like!" he blurted, his voice rising with each word. "Why, just this morning I was looking out the window and he was fine, and ten minutes later I started out to the kennel and he falls over on his side and just lies there."

"Was he floppin' around?" Arty asked.

"Floppin'?" Enos said. "No sir, he was as still as could be except for. . . ." He stopped.

"Except for what?" Arty persisted.

Enos massaged the furrows above his eyebrows. "Except for his tail. He was waggin' his tail."

"Wagging!" Mike roared. "He passed out and his tail was wagging?"

Enos nodded. "Is that bad?"

"Well, heck no, it's not bad, Enos," Arty said. "And it proves once and for all that a bird dog can reason. Everyone knows how pleased dogs are with dead fish and garbage and such. 'Ol Jobe got a taste of that mouth–to–mouth business and he liked it! Now he's pretending to pass out every chance he gets just to get a whiff of your breath!"

The laughter exploded in the room like a fireworks finale, looped around the wood stove, swung from the overhead fan, and slid down the walls. Slowly, very slowly, it crawled panting across the floor and under a pile of oily rags, but every five seconds or so, a new chuckle would sneak out and start up the wall again. To Enos's credit, he took the ribbing well, but when he left, he still maintained there was no such animal as a dog that reasoned. We did notice, though, he started buying breath mints shortly thereafter.

We also noticed Jobe made a complete recovery.

Pinto protocol

My friend, Gary, has spent over $1500 to have his black Lab, Bum, trained by a professional handler. Bum, he tells me, is now a hunting machine—steady to wing and shot, close working, soft–mouthed, and birdy as all get out. As might be expected from a man who would invest that kind of money in a dog he rescued from the pound, Gary has developed an anomalous affection for the dog's handler, putting the guy in his will and setting up a college trust for his children. I told Gary I'd do the same and throw in my collection of moose dropping cuff links for anyone who could teach my animals some vehicle etiquette; I worry more about Dude and Sundy embarrassing me in the car than in the field, a concern with every dog I've ever owned.

Though I enjoy my times alone, I seldom go bird hunting without a companion because it is comforting to share fantastic shots and unbelievable misses with an individual who has been there and appreciates both. Usually, then, when it is my turn to drive, the back seat is loaded with gear and dogs, and the passenger seat is occupied, sometimes by an old friend, sometimes a new one. Because it is my car, that makes me a program director of sorts, and the responsibility for an enjoyable day is in my hands. Unfortunately, my dogs choose to ignore these social obligations.

Sundy is the worst because she insists on staring out the window as I drive to the hunting area. Not caring much for the view out the back, she invariably rests her head on the shoulder of my partner for the day and drools heavily on his coat as she surveys the road ahead. This alone would not be too bad, but Sundy gets car sick, and she often forgets to remove her head when overcome with the urge to take another look at her last meal.

Dude is younger than Sundy, but wise enough to know that he, too, suffers from motion sickness, so he remains inert on the seat until we hit gravel. When he feels the tires crunching, however, he knows we are getting close, and rising to all fours, throws back his head and begins to sing. This doggy solo, which can best be described as "unnerving," lasts until we uncase our guns. Imagine a wolf with a toothache howling underwater and you get a general idea of the anguished warble emanating from Dude's hairy throat. The frequency is just loud enough to make your fillings hurt, but hunting partners being what they are, mine seldom say anything about the annoyance. Rather, they (especially the new ones) will ride along with their eyes bulging, making small talk and pretending they are entirely accustomed to having a tone–deaf canine sing in their ear. Rather than slap Dude on the nose as I suggest, some will share their entire lunch with him—a piece at a time—just to keep him quiet. Dude has a difficult time singing with his mouth full of corn chips and pickled herring.

One way or another, Mike usually loses his lunch to my dogs. On more occasions than I care to recount, he has forfeited his liverwurst sandwiches when Sundy and Dude were left locked in the car while he and I snuck a flock of ducks spotted from a back road. Though this is particularly upsetting to a man like myself who has a proclivity for forgetting his own lunch, thus counting on the generosity of companions for nourishment, I figure it is better than having the critters chew on the upholstery. Britt, my second dog, once ate $300 worth of sheepskin seat covers while my friend, Mark, and I had breakfast. Luckily for me, it was Mark's car.

Britt, bless his heart, hated to be left alone. I knew a place close to home where one could drive to the tops of some decent blue grouse ridges. The shooting there wasn't fantastic, but a small flock always seemed to be resting beneath a certain spruce snag—a comparatively easy walk and a nice way to end the day. The last time I went there, I left Britt in the car, figuring I was doing him a favor after a productive but strenuous workout that had netted two ruffs. Evidently, though, Britt wasn't impressed by my benevolence, and in his attempts to get out and join me, he knocked the car out of gear. When I returned, it was 600 yards down hill, nestled comfortably against a slab of granite with a rearranged front end. The dog? Britt was fine. I left him there on the front seat while I hiked out, and when I returned with the tow truck, he was just polishing off the second grouse.

The Christmas sequoia

According to my friend and hunting buddy, Seward Heaps, who is also a successful local psychologist, instances of suicides, domestic violence, and other destructive behavior increase ten–fold during the Christmas season. Seward, who is forever trying to either debate or enter into "meaningful dialogue" with his two Brittany spaniels, both of which have funnier names than he, is not by nature the jolliest of souls, but he does command a whole lot of attention from his clientele in the big city. Here where I live, however, we have rejected his broad "Holiday Depression Theory" which has a lot of variables and requires several cases of ten–dollar words to explain. We know that winter wackiness can actually last until spring and that the Christmas tree is the sole perpetrator.

Hundreds of Christmas holidays annually end in tears and ruin because we insist on putting large evergreens in our houses to celebrate the season. As ridiculous as this custom is, it should still be nothing more than a seasonal annoyance ending shortly after the Rose Bowl. In my house and apparently many others, however, the negative effects last until Memorial Day and involve five separate stages of annoyance: (1) finding the tree (2) getting it home (3) putting it up (4) putting it up again, and (5) getting rid of it. Any of these steps are capable of causing the depression and anger my friend Seward speaks of.

Few of us bother anymore to cut a "free" wild tree because

we can't afford it. After figuring the cost of a permit, a 240–mile round trip in a gas–guzzling 4x4, towing fees for extracting this same vehicle from the snow or mud, and possible legal fees for mistakenly cutting on private land, a single "free" tree can easily reach four figures. No, most Christmas trees are now purchased off lots in town by individuals who don't know for sure if they're getting a Scotch pine or a Russian olive because every tree on the lot has been sheared to look the same. A buyer *should* be able to stop at any lot, plop down $35.95, and take home an acceptable tree. In my house, however, Christmas tree *shopping* is a tradition carried over from my wife's childhood, and unless we stop and browse and haggle and freeze to death at a minimum of ten lots, we can't possibly find an acceptable tree or enjoy the season.

Once the tree has been located, admired, criticized, and argued over, it must be brought home. There just isn't an alternative. I have suggested to Lacey and the kids we could save a lot of hassles including clean–up and disposal, by taking our ornaments and lights to the lot where we made the purchase and setting up there, but none of them think it would be very "Christmasy" to put our packages under the dining room table and go down town when we have the urge to watch needles fall from an expensive evergreen. For that reason, we, like millions of other Americans, are obliged to carry home our sacred symbol using the car we came in—the one barely big enough for a driver and two sacks of groceries. With a little discretion concerning tree height, this would be manageable, but as I mentioned, my wife is into tradition, and a traditional family is not satisfied with less than a ceiling–sized conifer. Even this isn't too bad, though, unless the ceiling is 18 feet high—and ours is. I have suggested we put up a tree in the bathroom which has a standard eight–foot ceiling, but my wife fixes me with one of her dreaded "If–you–had–a–brain–you'd–take–it–out–and–play–with–it" looks, and each year I am obliged to bring home the sequoia on top of the car. This is rather like a first–grader giving a piggy–back ride to his father. It is also the ultimate challenge for a man who was kicked out of Cub Scouts without any knot–tying instruction because the den mother thought the neckerchief slide he was carving looked suspiciously like "heaving bosoms." Last year, the tree became independent of the car and I drug it several miles before I could get off the Interstate. Except for a few branches on one side, it would have made a pretty fair javelin. The year before, the tree was captured by a strong gust of wind that spun

it around perpendicular to the car and then rotated it a few times like the rotors of a helicopter until the ropes twisted tight and snapped, flinging our Yuletide greenery into the path of a Campbell's Soup semi.

Occasionally, I do get a tree home, and then wish I hadn't, for once the tree is through the door, it must go up. Thirty years ago, this was merely difficult; today, it is like trying to assemble a child's Hot Wheels track with no instructions, no tools, no degree in advanced engineering, and a three–hour deadline. Thirty years ago, Christmas trees came with sparse branches and thin trunks that sometimes actually fit in their stands. Today's Christmas tree, however, is not only sheared, it is "cultured," which means it is raised in a refined environment at a boarding school for evergreens. There, it eats and drinks prodigiously and never says anything politically incorrect. When it is harvested, it has a fat trunk and is four times heavier than its distant cousin who is still hanging out with the bears in the woods and will still have most of its needles on Christmas morning.

Fat–trunked trees do not fit in Christmas tree stands unless the trunks are whittled down, and tree stands built for wild trees will not hold fat ones with whittled–down trunks no matter how hard you twist those little screws on the bottom. Try reducing a cultured trunk to workable dimensions, and you end up with a Christmas tree that is like a time bomb waiting to go off. While you, your spouse, and your children argue over such important considerations as whether tinsel should be placed or tossed, the tree is thinking about its imminent detonation. Usually, this occurs right after the angel is attached, though sometimes a particularly devious one will wait until you have company over, or worse yet, until Christmas eve when the family gathers to open gifts and share in the magic of the night. There is nothing more unChristmasy on Christmas Eve than a tree lying in the middle of the living room with a bunch of crushed ornaments beneath it. No matter who gets the blame or what labors are expended on its resurrection, a tree that must be righted after a fall never looks quite finished because half the ornaments are shattered and the lights don't work. In my parents' house, I can remember one sorry evergreen that didn't go back up at all. My father, a very busy man who believed strongly in self–reliance calmly surveyed the devastation and said, "Let the blank–of–a–blank lie. If it wants to get up bad enough, it will."

Despite the protests of every child in the household, a mere two or three weeks after finally achieving conifer perpendicularity, the Christmas tree is intentionally brought down again, usually losing the last handful of needles and several more "they've–been–in–the–family–for–centuries" ornaments in the process. Pulled ingloriously across the carpet to the front door, followed by wailing sons and daughters pleading for "just one more month," the withered specimen is tossed into the front yard. "We'll deal with it later," I proclaim, but several months go by, and in March, Lacey sweetly suggests, "That mess better darn well be out of my flower bed by spring or I'll hire a man to pick it up." I, who have been trying to balance the budget ever since the Christmas buying frenzy, reject this idea and insist we can save money by disposing of the tree ourselves. I have heard all sorts of creative methods of Christmas tree disposal and have decided to take it to the local arboretum where the city has promised to grind ex–Christmas trees into mulch for use in decorative pathways.

In late May, however, the "tree," still suffering from good intentions, has only been moved as far as a cluttered spot behind the garage, the arboretum is no longer accepting donations, the two–week burning period is long past, and my spouse is once again complaining. Now, though, the "mess" has been officially designated an "eyesore." I tie the remains precariously atop a still–too–small car and drive to the county incinerator where a five dollar fee will somehow make the resulting smoke less offensive. The last six months have been a roller coaster of emotion, but, though scarred, my family has once more survived the looming presence of an 18–foot evergreen. By the following December, only the good parts will be remembered, and check book in hand, Lacey and I will bravely venture forth to begin the six–month cycle again.

When times were tough

Recently, Lacey's six–year–old nephew, Makka, came to stay with us while his parents attended a three–day parenting class in another city. Makka, whose name in Polynesia, means something like "Little one who puts poi in his eyebrows," is a red–headed, freckle–faced Irish–American with the last name Malone. He should have been called Mike or Patrick, and that is what I would have suggested had I been asked, which I wasn't. To me, "Makka" sounds like what a baby would say after trying to change his own diapers and making a mess of it.

When Makka and his mother first entered the house with his suitcases, I figured perhaps Lacey had adopted the little guy instead of merely agreeing to watch him for a few days. As a kid, when I was shipped off to relatives' homes for a weekend, I carried my clothes in a small paper sack. Except for my fishing pole, anything else of importance was in my front or back pockets.

"Whatcha got in the suitcases, Mackey?" I said when his mother had left and he stood forlornly at the window with his little tongue making slobbery swirls, first on an orange popsicle and then on the glass pane.

He turned his head to study me critically, and after a quick evaluation, sighed. "My name is Makka," he announced importantly. "What's there to do?"

Before I could answer, he sat down on the living room

carpet and opened the first of his two extremely large pieces of luggage. From it he extracted two hand–held video games, an AM/FM stereo, a dual cassette recorder with a five band graphic equalizer, a battery–operated automobile with pivoting front axle, and a pair of fluorescent–green in–line skates. In the other suitcase were some clothes and about 5,000 batteries.

"So, Melvin," I said, "it looks to me like there's plenty to do right here. If nothing else, we could put together a garage sale, heh, heh." I was going to say "Har–dee–har–har," but remembered his generation does not appreciate Jackie Gleason and as a whole, remains pathetically uncharmed by humor more subtle than an "American Home Video" episode in which a fat man with plumber's butt swings at a golf ball, misses, rolls down a hill, and breaks his leg.

Lacey's nephew fixed me with a sympathetic stare but said nothing. Instead, he shook his head slowly a couple times, rolled his eyes, and sat down cross–legged on the living room carpet where he began to compete with an electronic video game in which space aliens were trying to blow up Los Angeles. I watched quietly several minutes, rooting for the space aliens, but it became evident the lad was engrossed in something beyond my realm of comprehension, inclination, and level of dexterity. I had just decided I would get more enjoyment out of the day if I went out and watched the dandelions grow, when he dropped the miniature computer in mid–game and began playing with a remote–controlled car. Almost immediately, it climbed over my shoe like a big turtle and began crawling up my leg. As I prepared to demonstrate my displeasure by whacking it with a rolled up newspaper, little Mason shut off the juice to his personal Christine and it thudded lifelessly to the floor. Except for the two small tread marks on my shin, I was unscathed. "What's there to do now, Uncle?" he asked.

Naturally, I thought he was being facetious. Not counting batteries, the child had nearly a quarter–million dollars in toys spread out on the carpet. How could he possibly want for something to do? I flashed quickly to my own childhood when sharpening popsicle sticks by rubbing them on the sidewalk

was considered high entertainment. The fact those sharpened popsicle sticks later had absolutely no function was irrelevant. It was something to do I could afford, and I derived motivation enough from the fact there was a sidewalk and I had a stick.

"Well?" Mortimer was tapping his foot impatiently, having mistaken my reflection for contemplation of his personal dilemma.

"I'm thinking, kid," I shot back, and I was. I was thinking of 1951 when I was six years old and times were tough. I was thinking about my ten–cent–a–week allowance and how my parents cared not a whit about keeping up with the Joneses because they hadn't even caught up to the Grabowskis who were the second–poorest folks on the block.

Mostly, kids' entertainment in those days had but one criteria: it had to be cheap; and though a dearth of funds *can* foster creativity, most creative six–year–olds would be better off in a detention facility for small people. Some of my own activities back then would have earned me at least a month's worth of professional psychological evaluation today, and perhaps some juridical intervention besides.

One of those questionable activities involved Harley Collett's water dogs—salamander–like creatures he raised in a defunct ringer washer and used for bass bait. Sometimes, Harley went off to work at the mill and forgot to lock his garage door, an oversight we six–year–olds viewed as a welcome mat. Obviously, we reasoned, Harley wanted the denizens of his washing machine exercised, and we knew there was nothing quite as good for flushing water dog cholesterol as a 20–foot dash down a cement sidewalk. Thus, the Queen Street Water Dog Races evolved.

To this day, I have not determined why we felt it was necessary to insert Harley's water dogs in empty boxes of Good 'n Plenty, Dots, or Ju Jus before racing, but we did. With their heads poking out one end, their tails out the other, and their stubby little legs sticking through holes punched in the bottoms of the boxes, his salamanders would race down the cement to glorious victory or dismal defeat, looking for all the world like zany, animated candy advertisements. Sadly, my father put an end to this activity when old Mrs. Bruinmeister, who was returning a cup of borrowed molasses, threw out her hip in an inelegant, sticky retreat from what she hysterically described as "Dem turdles wid da long tails!"

Digging was another activity that occupied a lot of time when times were tough. In fact, years before I ever picked up a shotgun, I had been practicing digging goose pits which, when covered with twigs and weeds, became very adequate big game traps. One day, when there was a shortage of water buffalo in the neighborhood, I lured my sometimes friend, Lucy, into a game of "Follow the leader," intent on getting her wet by leading her along the path and over my "trap," which I had filled with water. If the reader finds this admission despicable, the reader must be reminded the books from which I took the idea actually suggested sharpened bamboo stakes rather than water. Luckily for Lucy, it didn't make any difference; she was too light to break through the covered pit on the first pass, and I had to lead her on a circular route which brought us by a second time. When the twigs *again* refused to break, I tried them out myself, finding my weight to be exactly enough to plummet me through to the bottom. Thus, I was soggily reminded that creativity and intelligence were not synonymous.

"Uncle Alan." There was a tugging on my pant leg, but it was way too low to be Lacey who always went for the pocket change first. "Uncle Alan!" Malabaar was still there, looking more bored than ever. "What are we going to do?"

"Hold your horses, kid," I told him. "I'm still thinking." I had just remembered the *ne plus ultra* of all tough–times activities:

A city kid, my life finally became meaningful one summer when my folks let me stay at my Uncle Verlyn's cattle ranch for a week. For my part, I could have gone on catching those small bluegill from the farm pond, squirting the barn cats with fresh, warm milk, and searching for those warm, brown eggs the rest of my life. My cousins, Calvin and Lester, however, had become so accustomed to these activities they quickly grew bored, and when a ranch hand gave them several packs of Fourth of July firecrackers, they invented a game they called "cow pie chicken" and challenged me to join them. The rules were simple: The three of us would approach the largest, freshest cow pie in the pasture. Kneeling around it just inches away, we'd stick a single firecracker deep into the "pie" and light it. The first to run was the "chicken." Simple, cheap, and messy—perfect for a kid when times were tough.

My reflections winding down, I turned my attention to Lacey's nephew. "Morphus," I called. "Morphus? I was thinking maybe we could get some firecrackers and you could. . . ." Through the screened door I heard a vaguely familiar sound coming from the front step. "Morphus," I called, stepping outside. "I. . .hello. . .What's this? Well, I'll be darned! Popsicle sticks? You're what? Sharpening them? Whatever for, Makka? 'Zat so, huh? You don't know. Makes sense to me. You know, Makka my lad, I did a little of that myself when I was your age and. . . .What's that? Why of course I'd like to join you. Say, lad, did I ever tell you how much I admired your name? I didn't? Well, Makka, I do. When I was a child my parents called me Scooter. Of course, I didn't have that itch forever, but. . . ."

Toys!

Chasen Bean, a friend of mine from college, recently stopped by the house to show off some of his new toys. Chasen's wife, it seems, had gone a little hog–wild during one of those pre–Christmas sales at a local boutique, and to make a point, Chasen, who is every man's handyman, had retaliated in Foo's Hardware. Included in his spending spree were a multiple–speed drill, a set of metric socket wrenches, a router, and a couple miles of extension cord. After viewing his toys, of course, I was obligated to drag out a few of my own, but being as interested in building and fixing as I am in gastronitis and knitting, my toys leaned heavily toward shooting and angling accessories. I think Chasen was most impressed by the one–man clay pigeon thrower, but had he known anything at all about fishing, he would have drooled when I brought out my 7 1/2–foot, heat–tempered bamboo fly rod.

My infatuation with toys, I know, stems from a childhood tainted by the taste of liver and Lima beans. There were precious few luxuries in our household during my first ten years, and even at Christmas, my parents thought putting food (in any form) on the table more important than putting whimsical presents under the tree. Because of this convoluted precept, it didn't take more than 30 seconds or so Christmas morning to open my package. Usually, I received socks, period, which were warm, practical, boring, and at least partially responsible for so fracturing my self esteem it took all the king's horses and all the king's men many years to put it together again. My teacher's said it also made me weird. My wife says it still does.

When my eight–year–old friends were trying out new sleds, shooting new B–B guns, or cleaning one another out in Monopoly, my only entertainment was to hide in my bedroom, taking my new socks off and putting them back on, pretending they were Roy Rogers cowboy boots or even shiny roller skates from the window of North Hill Drug. Later, I might wad them into a ball and shoot baskets over at Franklin Park, and when no one was looking, sit shoeless on the front porch making a variety of guttural "shooting" sounds with my mouth while "gunning down" passing airplanes and sparrows with my stockinged big toe. Indeed, it was there on the porch I formulated my first theories concerning lead, swing, follow through, and the wicking superiority of wool over nylon.

As the years went by, my parents' diligence and thrift began to pay off where it counted—under the Christmas tree, and when I was 12, there were TWO packages for me on that special morning. One, of course, contained socks to remind me of my roots, and I opened that first, gave the obligatory thank yous and kisses, and set it aside. The other, a very large box wrapped lovingly in the colorful Sunday paper comic section and tied with blue ribbon salvaged from my last birthday present (so I would remember "Waste not, want not") contained a complete, plastic, snap–together log stockade along with assorted plastic Indians, cowboys, and horses, all in a variety of action–packed and menacing poses. Now this was more like it! Toys!!

For 197 days straight, my parents now insist, I messed with that stockade, playing out every normal scenario imaginable and some that made my mother shake her head and question the mental stability of my father who had contributed half the genes in this strange child she had borne. In the early stages, plastic Indians riding plastic horses attacked plastic cowboys with plastic grins who hid behind plastic walls. Later, the cowboys launched a counter–attack, and later still, the cowboys and the Indians merged and bought out a feed store. Soon afterwards, however, the horse–employees went on strike and when the business fell apart, the owners became enemies again. In one of my greatest battles, horses riding atop cowboys attacked a small band of unarmed Indians who were holed up in the stockade practicing headstands, but they were repelled by Benny Winkleman's plastic G.I.s who had hidden themselves inside with hand grenades and bazookas. Boy were those horses surprised!

With Christmas just around the corner this year, Lacey and the kids are once again wondering what I have on my wish list. Sure, I need a new dress shirt, my belt has shrunk again, and I never did get the salmon egg oil and Tobasco off my lone tie. But I never have forgotten the the thrill of that plastic stockade, either. Toys!! That's what's on my Christmas list. Binoculars, a spotting scope, and a 42–tray tackle box. An electronic collar for the dog and a gun rack for the truck. A new shell vest in fluorescent camo and an electric, diamond–hone knife sharpener.

Oh, yeah. . . and socks. One pair. Cotton. White. To remind me of my roots.

The extended lull

Cautiously, Eddie poked his head from the blind, squinting his eyes against a ten o'clock sun and scanning the sky for movement. Nothing. It was a bright, bluebird, December morning and the ducks weren't flying. Every 15 minutes since dawn, he had repeated the ritual, but so far the only excitement had come early when an owl swooped out of a stand of aspen to investigate our decoys. "This," Eddie said, as he settled back into the reeds, "is what they call a lull."

An hour later, a leaking hip boot was making me numb all over and I snuggled further into the down parka that had seemed so unnecessary an hour earlier. Eddie, though, was on his feet, shading his eyes as he scanned the horizon. "And this," he said, "is what they call an extended lull."

By noon we had consumed two lunches and a gallon of coffee and I was trying to peel the cellophane wrapper from a crushed, miniature candy cane I'd found in my shirt pocket. The fact it had gone unnoticed through a half dozen washes since the previous Christmas intrigued me and made my unwrapping endeavors delightfully time–consuming. Eddie stared at me enviously as I picked away.

"You always have the most fun," he finally said. "Got any more of those?"

A thorough search failed to turn up additional candy canes, and Eddie wasn't interested in the pack of Life–Savers I dug from my duffel bag. "I'm not hungry," he admitted, "I'm bored. Tell you what. . . Let me finish picking the cellophane off that one and when I'm done, I'll give you the candy."

Anyone can enjoy themselves in a duck blind when the ducks are in, and sporadic action provided by a small flock, or even a single every hour or so, is sufficient to keep most waterfowlers shivering in anticipation. What these individuals do on a duckless day, however, is the incontrovertible measure of dedication to the sport. Picking up and going home would be the intelligent thing to do, but finding innovative means of killing flightless hours separates duck hunters from duck shooters, and duck *hunters*, by the very nature of their chosen sport, are a few pellets shy of a load.

After all the bad jokes, tired stories and strong coffee; after the blind has been repaired, enlarged, and decorated with dried weed arrangements; after the lunches are eaten and shells have been categorized by shot size, color, and approximate age, real duck hunters must settle in for an extended lull. During this period, ranging anywhere from one to seven hours, they must be prepared to kill time.

Killing time is defined as doing something while doing nothing. In duck hunting, it is an activity that occupies body and mind with anything but the reality that the duck dinner you promised your relatives is still rafted in the middle of the largest reservoir in the state. Killing time is difficult for the novice, but anyone used to routinely explaining away alarm clocks that ring an hour late, wrong turns taken, and missed shots, should have no difficulty entertaining themselves in a duck blind.

If music is the universal language, a duck blind during a lull is the amphitheater. It is amazing how many long–forgotten tunes from my youth are instantly recalled when the birds aren't flying. It is equally amazing how well a fine–tuned duck or goose call compliment my singing. "Does your chewing gum lose its flavor on the bedpost overnight—quack, quack. . If your mother says don't chew it do you swallow it in spite—quack, honk. . .Do you hang it on your tonsils and heave it left and right—honk, honk. . .Does your chewing gum lose its

flavor on the bedpost overnight? Quackety–quack–quack, honk honk!"

It must be noted here that a good singing voice is not absolutely necessary to participate in this uplifting time–killer. In fact, it is more a liability than an asset, as too much timbre and resonance will discourage hunting buddies from joining in for fear of not meeting expectations. The goal is to involve everyone in the blind. In the event, however, they are completely overwhelmed by your vocal exactitude, it is important to remember duck and goose calls alone are adequate for conveying the magic of music and in gobbling up the long hours between flights. My personal rendition of "There's a Place in France," done solely on a Yentzen double–reed mallard call is a slack–hour favorite, and when accompanied by an occasional "ha–ronk" from a buddy's goose call, it approaches art.

Making obscene noises with my boots in the mud underfoot is another way I wile away flightless hours, usually saving it until my singing voice begins to crack. It's not art, I admit, but I'm enthralled by the way different ratios of earth to water create such a variety of slurps and sucking sounds. Sometimes, these are even combined with quacks and honks. "Your Cheatin' Heart" was never performed the way Eddie and I can do it with two pairs of size 12s, a duck call, a goose call, and a lot of hysterical laughter.

Unfortunately, there comes a time between the second and fourth hour of an extended lull that entertainment characterized by levity gives way to a consuming desire to irritate the hunting partner who dragged me out of bed at three a.m. to participate in such futility. Never mind that it was my idea in the first place. A short lapse of memory is a time–honored means for transferring blame and for killing time.

Staring is a common technique for causing irritation, and it doesn't matter what I'm staring at, even if it's nothing: "What are you looking at?" the person next to me will ask as I fix and hold my gaze on the mud floor of the blind. In such instances, I've found a slow, knowing, smile—one that makes me look like I have gas—will accentuate the aggravation. If you've seen enough Jack Nicholson movies to have perfected his insane grin and his "I'm–going–to–kill–you" eyes, the aggravation approaches terror. If you're staring at your buddy, his discomfort is compounded immeasurably.

Pounding a spent shotgun shell from a previous hunt into the dirt wall of a pit blind with the teaspoon I've brought to eat my butterscotch pudding, is both entertaining and aggravating enough to offer satisfaction. Pounding the same casing into my partner's arm is sure to liven up a no–duck morning.

If there is no action by the fifth hour, I begin sniffing. There is something about prolonged sniffing that can nauseate even the most hardened hunter, and I find it interesting to note its effects on my blind–mate. I have seen men who can skin a coyote on a hot afternoon, gag after being exposed to prolonged sniffing. Sniffing is easy, does not necessarily require a runny nose, and is capable of providing up to three hours of entertainment before your partner catches on and begins sucking his teeth in retaliation.

My friend, Eddie, has devised another means for counteracting my sniffing, and though I find it hateful, wish I'd thought of it first: "Get down!" he'll yell at irregular intervals after the fifth hour. The hope is that I will assume a flock of mallards has snuck in from behind and will make a fool of myself diving for the floor of the blind. What usually happens, though, is I first spill the coffee I was pouring and *then* make a fool of myself diving for the floor of the blind. Because I am not overly coordinated, this ruse always works, even if I'm standing *in* the blind; it's more entertaining, however, if I'm *outside* of it.

Fortunately, fifth–hour deviousness usually runs its course and is replaced by more routine forms of entertainment, like picking the wax from your ears with a weed stem or counting the hairs on your fingers. A variation of this activity is counting the hairs on your buddy's fingers, but this should never be done while he is awake, and you should refrain from holding his hand while you count.

The hours between noon and dusk are, without reservation, the toughest during an extended lull. Anticipation has given away to resignation: "We're here, so we might as well stick it out." At such times, a creative hunting partner with a sense of humor is of more value than a good dog and a gun that shoots true. Eddie is that kind of guy. While his behavior would draw stares on downtown streets, it's exactly what is needed to get me through a no–show afternoon.

Last hunting season, Eddie and I had suffered together on a small pond south of town—a rainy, windy, perfect–for–duck day that hadn't been. For some reason, waterfowl avoided our decoys by the hundreds. By two p.m., no shots had been fired.

"Well, that does it," Eddie said, climbing out of the cave we'd created in the reeds on the pond's west side. "I was hoping I wouldn't have to resort to this, but they've left me no choice." With that, he placed a partially–deflated rubber decoy on his head, assumed a duck–walk position, and waddled down to the water. "Here duck! Here duck!" he called as I doubled over with laughter.

At that moment, a huge flock of northerns—big, bright mallards—popped over the tops of the surrounding trees and settled without circling, 20–yards in front of us. Grabbing my shotgun, I stood up just as Eddie swiveled around, crossed his eyes, stuck a finger in his nose, and shrugged. The sight of a 50–year–old stockbroker hunkered at water's edge looking like Red Skelton's Clem Kadiddlehopper with a decoy on his head, was too much, and I resumed my hysterical shrieking. The mallards, of course, took off, looking back in puzzlement, but I didn't care. Heck, we still had several hours of light, and sometimes an extended lull is more fun than a good shoot.

Clammin'

When I was a toddler, my favorite medium of expression was a soupy mixture of loam and water. My parents called me "Mr. Mud," because according to them, you could set me down on an expanse of soft, green turf and surround me with store–boughten toys, and in no time at all I'd be playing with the hose in the flower bed, creating mud pies, cakes, castles, and condominiums. Most likely, this inclination was the result of a damaged chromosome, but Lacey says it is additional evidence of my congenital exigency to be aberrant. There's no way a woman who talks like that and changes socks each day can appreciate a place like Clam Gulch, Alaska.

Clam Gulch was created on the swing shift when God realized man could not live on salmon alone. He had already spent hours creating forests, mountains, rivers, and gift shops, and then had to work overtime to provide some sandy beaches where a man could wander, reflecting on why the 49th state received so many extra handfuls of splendor. Across the water from Clam Gulch, three active volcanoes—Mts. Spurr, Redoubt, and Iliamna—thrust nearly two miles into the sky, overseeing activities on Cook Inlet. Clam diggers find the mountains' magnificence magnetic, and many spend as much time photographing as they do moving sand. Personally, I prefer moving sand.

The fact is, I still like to get dirty. There is something delicious about crusted fingernails, grimy jeans, and the squish of mud in my tennis shoes. I derive a certain smugness from knowing at Monday business luncheons where I must wear a tie and eat with a fork, that I looked like a demented mud wrestler on Sunday. That is why I most like to dig razor clams at Clam Gulch, Alaska. No other activity I can think of offers quite so many opportunities to forget completely who you are and how you're *supposed* to act. Clammin' lets you be a kid again.

Razor clams and I have this thing about muddy sand—we love it. Though I have experienced a trauma or two driving on a beach, the therapeutic qualities outweigh inconveniences. What man can ignore the beckoning expanse of utter smoothness, the temptation to race along the edge of an ocean highway uncluttered with stop lights or yellow lines? Not I. Unlike snow drifts, which I also appreciate, and which have an incredible attraction for my vehicles, Clam Gulch sand is unforgiving—it has no bottom. One can get really dirty digging there and still be stuck when the sun goes down, the tow truck arrives, or the tide comes in. Burying my vehicle to the doors is part of clammin' in Alaska, and I look upon it as my contribution to the economy of the Kenai Peninsula. It is my fantasy that the families of tow truck operators enjoy a little merrier Christmas each year because I came briefly into their lives.

The clamming season in Alaska, a year–long affair, was established by the powers that be to save tax dollars. At one time, there was concern in certain resorts and fishing communities that shifting beach sand would necessitate major dredging operations in the harbors. Every clam digger, according to recent statistics, carries an average of 12 pounds of sand and mud back to his home or motel—under his fingernails, ground into the knees of his pants, lining the inside of his tennis shoes. Another 15 pounds is plastered to the undercarriage of his car. In a few more years, this transfer of sand will make the problem of harbor siltation non–existent. Then, Peninsula chambers of commerce will begin giving tourists complimentary devil's club, and the coastal region will have economically eliminated its two greatest scourges.

While getting to the clam beds can be traumatic, the actual process of digging the razor clam is high comedy. The elliptical–shaped Siliqua patula reveals his position by drawing in his siphon (neck) when the tide ebbs. This creates a brief waterspout which leaves a small indentation or dimple in the sand. On my first venture into clam country I didn't know this; I merely walked out on the beach and began to dig. After two hours, I had excavated an area roughly the size of a football stadium without turning a shell and was flirting with cardiac arrest complicated by severe skin abrasions. It was not until later I learned razor clams are not dug at high tide. In succeeding weeks, I also learned that experienced clammers consider it outrageously funny to stand by without saying a word while a maverick ocean wave engulfs the novice digger who has ventured too close to the water and turned his back. To this day, one of my most cherished memories is the look of fear, determination, and resignation on the face of my brother–in–law when he touched his first burrowing razor clam and realized in that same instant the roar he heard behind him was created by the wave about to break over his back.

The best digging for razor clams is in muddy sand, and once the shoveling begins, the bi–valve punches "Basement" on the fast elevator. I have my most consistent success by taking three quick scoops directly over a dimple, then throwing my shovel aside and plunging into the hole with both arms. Though some feel throwing the shovel is optional, it is not. The distance of the toss, in fact, is a barometer of enthusiasm and signals the body to pump more adrenalin. A good shovel toss can accelerate the capture of a clam by as much as 30 seconds. Sometimes, also, if one does not maintain an awareness of his proximity to the sea, it serves as an offering to the god, Neptune.

Once the arms are buried to the elbows, the main thing to remember is you must get as dirty as possible. This is not optional, either. A razor clam is awed by an individual who is not afraid to lie on his side in the sand and muck and extend his arm past the clavicle, and oft–times, the mollusk will stop his own excavating just to get a good look at his gutsy pursuer. If this should occur and something hard is touched, one must refrain from prematurely making the triumphant announcement that "I've got one!" It may be a clam, but it may also be a rock or the distributor cap to a '49 Ford. It is unnecessary to provide veteran diggers with the impetus for additional mirth.

Razor clams should be cleaned as soon after capture as possible, preferably by someone else. The process requires a surgeon's understanding of anatomy, and it often takes longer than the pursuit. The neck is tough and best chopped and saved for chowder or used whole as an eraser, but the body and "foot" are tender and delicious. I have heard of individuals who will bread and fry these in butter, consuming a dozen at a sitting, but in my house, they are rationed. When I figure gas, towing, and dry cleaning, razor clams cost over 50 bucks a pound. Lacey says it would be cheaper for me to send hired diggers after the clams. Then, I could stay home and play with the hose in the flower bed.

Dear Max:

As I recall, on your last visit you left Loon Lake in a head–lock; I trust you and your mom have since resolved at least a few of your differences. Telephone calls, homework, and the apparent misuse of weekends are rather predictable sources of parent–child conflicts, Max, but if I were you, I would strongly consider the consequences before again challenging Marsha's intelligence *or* her authority. Your mother is one of the finest people I know—my favorite cousin—and she loves you too much to let you think disrespect has no consequences. Besides that, it appears she still remembers some of the wrestling holds she used on *me* when we were kids.

Personally, when I was 15, I never had any of the problems you are currently experiencing. My folks locked me in my bedroom when I got my first hormone, and they didn't let me out until Lacey knocked on the window and asked me to marry her. Or something like that. You've got some good things going for you, Max—not the least of which are your genes; you come from good stock. When you are older, you'll be absolutely amazed at how intelligent your mom has become. You'll also wonder what happened to your hair, but I guess it's not my place to prepare you for all of life's surprises in one letter. Genes, after all, can be very tricky.

Was it just three seasons ago that we shivered together for the first time in that scab rock blind behind Howard Bunting's windmill? You thought *then* I knew everything about waterfowl hunting, and I was pleased to perpetuate the misconception, probably because I enjoyed being your hero. Actually, Max, there are some things I'm just *now* beginning to understand. I had intended to share these thoughts with you a couple weeks ago, but your inelegant departure messed things up.

If you recall, it was a few weeks ago that you asked me how many geese I'd killed on my last trip to Canada and I said I'd taken a half dozen or so. You seemed disappointed there hadn't been more, but the truth is, *I* was disappointed you had not asked the right questions. I know it is unreasonable, but I wanted you to ask about the land and the people, and all the other little things that make a hunt a hunt. I wanted to tell you about the golden stubble fields that stretched to the horizons. I wanted to describe how the tumbleweeds raced the rain clouds to town each afternoon, and then to paint verbal pictures of the congenial men and magnificent dogs that shared my blinds. I wanted you to ask if my heart beat twice as fast when there were twice as many birds, or if I talked to myself to keep from shouting with excitement when the "whoosh, whoosh" of their wings lifted the hair on the back of my neck.

You didn't ask me about the important stuff because you're 15-years old. I wanted you to, though—for both of us. I wanted you to because I, who should know better, forgot once that a hunting trip is not about numbers. I was far under my legal Canadian limit on this last trip, Max, and I feel real good about that. You remember when I told you about my first trip, though—the one when I burned three boxes of shells in five days. It wasn't that long ago. We were both pretty excited about it because I killed a lot of geese, but I killed something else up there on the prairies—something inside of me—and it took a long while to get it back. I killed the mystique, Max—the goose magic.

When I was a kid—perhaps a few years younger than you—I would go out on the porch when a flock of geese flew over, and

I would salute. Honest to God, Max, I would salute! Couldn't help myself. Wild geese always seemed so noble, so intrepid, so focused, and I was sure I was in the presence of something much greater than anything mere man could create. When I began waterfowl hunting, nothing changed. If anything, my admiration grew. Each goose was a gift to be cherished and enjoyed.

But one time I forgot, Max. I sat up there in those fancy blinds in Canada and I kept pulling the trigger, and after the first four or five, I didn't even look at those birds. Not really. I didn't turn them over in my hands, smooth the feathers, and feel the warmth. I didn't think about where they had come from or where they were going. Oh, it was all legal, and afterwards, I gave geese away to anyone who would have them. But it wasn't good. I killed the magic because there were more birds than I had ever seen at one time, and it was too easy. I didn't stop shooting nearly soon enough, and afterwards I felt dirty, like the blood on my hands had seeped into the pores and rotted. Don't ever let that happen to you, Max. Keep asking the right questions. To do this hunting thing right, a man has to remind himself of what he is doing and why he is doing it. He has to keep the respect. And don't forget to salute.

See you at the wild game dinner in April.

Alan

"Ma. . .there's a pig at the door!"

Though theories may differ, I have always felt hoarding is a primitive instinct rather than learned behavior. Hidden in the genetic composition of all men, it remains largely recessive in the 20th century, but like night blindness or schizophrenia, it can't be ignored when it rears its ugly head. The trick in keeping it dormant is to refrain from activating the gene in the first place. Don't, for example, ever freeze that first batch of home–grown strawberries or stash that first fireplace log in the carport. My former best friend, Cyril Moody, is a case in point, and were it not for my red longjohns, I might be also.

Cyril was an exasperating family man but an excellent buddy. Of all my friends, he was the only one who would put his other life on hold to accompany me on my spontaneous outdoor expeditions throughout the state. Good goose hunting out of Redfish Cove? Cyril and his 4x4 would pick me up at the house. Silvers hitting in Cedarbow Bay? Cyril and his boat could meet me at the dock in half an hour. Behind, he left a series of half–built decks, unmowed lawns, and partially–painted bedrooms. Sadly, however, there were no diversions the week Cyril installed his wood stove, and when the job was complete, I lost him forever to the clamorous song of a chainsaw.

While state laws, personal ethics, and poor reflexes minimized Cyril's hoarding of fish and game, nothing could stop him once he began cutting firewood. Cyril became a five, then a six, then a 10–cord–a–year man. Never mind that his stove burned only four cords each winter. Never mind that he sold his boat to make additional room for the fir and birch in the car port or that his back yard became a maze of stacked wood and blue tarps. There was no way Cyril could use all he had taken; he was cutting wood for the joy of seeing it accumulate.

Instead of shotguns and casting reels, Cyril began talking about maul weight and bar oil, topics I found even less stimulating than an exercise bike. He missed the grouse opener to "put in another cord," and even traded his 30.06 for a wood trailer. Finally, Cyril gave away his black Labrador retriever "so I can put a couple cords in the kennel," and that was the last straw; I tip–toed quietly out of his life. Sure, I had a wood stove—it came with the house—but I had been buying my fuel, and after my friend's convincing collapse, I decided my oil furnace would do me just fine in the future.

Despite this resolve, an unforseen circumstance early last spring caused me to re–evaluate my lifestyle—I lost my job. With expensive oil heat I could no longer afford accustomed luxuries like medication for my athletes foot or milk for my gruel. Reluctantly, I purchased a used chain saw and a cheap, red, hard hat, cleaned out my pickup bed, and made ready to become a wood cutter.

Although chain–sawing attire had never before been a consideration at my house, I assumed from what I had seen in others that grubbiness and tastelessness were priorities. No problem. For years I have maintained three separate wardrobes ranging from grubby to tasteless to "Alan, I threw that rag out six weeks ago. Why is it back in this house?" Choosing from the first two closets, I extracted a pair of short, plaid–green, polyester pants, a blue–checkered shirt covered with piling tar, and a pair of decrepit, low–cut, black tennis shoes that had never seen a court. Underneath it all went a red wool union suit I had once worn when attending a Halloween party dressed as a sow pig. It was musty from years of storage and badly moth–eaten, and the rear flap was stapled together, but what made it so distinctive were the two rows of Playtex baby bottle nipples I had glued to the chest. Though I briefly considered removing them, I figured the costume might someday be useful again, and it was unlikely anyone would notice them under my shirt. With no further thought, I donned the hardhat and drove toward Hannah Flats.

Despite my recalcitrance for the task at hand, the day progressed pleasantly. A mere 40 miles from home, I located a stand of dead black pine. The sun came out, the chainsaw performed admirably, and my truck was filling quickly. At noon, when I stopped for a sandwich and removed my hot, long–sleeved shirt, a black bear stared at me from just below the road, and somewhere in the forest behind, a ruffed grouse drummed on a log, sounding for all the world like an old tractor coming to life. Good stuff.

I resumed working a short time later, but even as the sun grew warmer, sweat burned my eyes, and the pickup overflowed, I did not stop cutting. The fresh aroma of wood pitch was like an elixer, and the clean, even cuts gave me a feeling of self–worth. Here, indeed, was something that made sense: I was surrounded by nature, I was saving money, and I was being revitalized both physically and emotionally. Frustrations, personal rejection, and other accumulated irritations disappeared in a fragrant cloud of pine chips and bar oil. Mental images of inept accountants, oafish government bureaucrats, and laughing tax auditors were ripped from the bark and sprayed into oblivion. Power. Control. Fleeting insanity. I was King For A Day; it was glorious. Shedding my long–sleeved shirt, I worked until dark, stockpiling for a second load.

On the way out, my truck complaining under the fruits of honest toil, I remembered the checkered shirt hanging over the stump where I had shed it. Oh well, I thought—I'll get it tomorrow. I adjusted my hardhat and drove on, happily oblivious to the six Playtex nipples jiggling playfully on my chest.

There is nothing subtle about a broken axle. "Clunk!" And that's all she wrote. It happened when I was barely out of the woods. Having the mechanical inclinations of a twine ball, I didn't even bother with an examination of the offending part.

My vehicle was broken. Eventually, it would get fixed, but it was not I who would perform this mechanical magic. I had learned many years before that socket wrenches and cold metal responded to neither pathetic whimpers nor angry threats. It was getting chilly, but in the distance I could see a light off in the trees, and I walked toward it hoping there would be a telephone and, at least, a little sympathy.

A dog barked as I walked up the gravel driveway and climbed the steps onto a long, railed porch. I knocked and then smiled amiably as a girl of about 12 pulled back the curtain and stared at my face through the glass. The door opened tentatively,

the light of the kitchen filling in the shadows. "Hi there," I began, "I've got a little prob. . . ."

"Maaaaa," she hollered over her shoulder, "there's a pig at the door!" Inside, there was a shuffling and a large, round woman came into view carrying her knitting under a beefy arm.

"Now stop that ruckus out here or. . . ." She stopped short of the threshhold, her eyes widening as the ball of yarn and two knitting needles fell to the linoleum. "Oh my. . .Oh my. . ." she sputtered. Then she shrieked loudly, "Hennn–reee!" and threw herself against the door. In seconds, her male clone rounded the corner of the house wielding a two–bitted axe.

"What the blazes are you women. . . ." He stopped short of the porch steps and gripped his weapon with both hands. "Ahright, fella," he said menacingly, "jus' hold 'er right there." He advanced cautiously. "Git off the porch," he ordered.

"But sir. . . ." I tried to explain, still unaware that it was my pig costume causing all the commotion.

"Don't say nothin', prevert," he growled, "lessen ya wants I should mash yer head with this here axe. Git off the porch and lay on the groun'!"

I complied, losing my hardhat in the process. "I suppose a cup of coffee is out of the question?" I said from my back, the gravel jabbing through my old red underwear.

"Don't say nothin'," the man repeated. He glared at me savagely. "An 'specially don't oink." He poked at me with the axe handle. "Ma," he said, "call Sheriff Hanks."

Eventually, the mess was cleared up, but not before I was treated to a night in a small–town hoosegow with an inebriated logger who reminded me of a character from the movie, Deliverance, and made me mighty nervous. When I was released the next morning, Sheriff Hanks graciously apologized and drove me to my truck where I discovered my entire load of wood had disappeared. He drove me home and I thanked him profusely, bought a raffle ticket for a cord of red fir, and assured him he should not look for me again in his jurisdiction until he saw the Devil wearing a Santa suit. When I got in the house, I phoned Holz Petroleum, disguised my voice, and ordered 500 gallons of heating oil on credit.

A decree of expectations

Choosing a big–footed, needle–toothed bundle of fur and energy from a six–week–old litter of eight and calling it your hunting dog is quite possibly the most optimistic thing a person will ever do. Taking it home to the family and attempting to agree on a name may be the toughest. A pup's name is a decree of expectations—not an endeavor to be lightly undertaken. It must reflect just the right amount of boldness, aggression, and stamina. It must hint at loyalty and affection and shout of obedience and heart. As a single man, I sometimes managed this responsibility in two or three days, but as a husband and father, it became a task only slightly less frustrating than my attempts to understand chess and feminine fashion codes.

I tried to impress upon my wife and progeny the importance of a hunting dog's name. One syllable, I told them, was ideal, but two was okay. Certainly not three. Of course, there would be a number of names automatically eliminated because of past associations. Dibs, for example, was a perfectly fine name for a dog, but as a boy, there was a Dibs on the block where I lived that gained a reputation of sorts and won several bets for his young master by gluttonously consuming anything placed before him, regardless of the consistency, stage of decomposition, or color. Dibs was given a wide berth by other neighborhood dogs, but whether this had to do with his personality or his breath, I did not know. I *did* know there would be no Dibs in my kennel.

Dog names, I reminded my family, originate from many sources. Rusty, Blackie, Brownie, and Goldie reflected colors, and though this technique for choosing a name was not overly sophisticated, it wasn't such a bad way to go. Some notable color exceptions for names were mauve, pea–green, and puce. Vermillion I liked, but it had too many syllables. Then, there were hunting dogs named after presidents. Abe, Zack, and Ike were solid examples, but other names weren't nearly as strong and needed to be avoided. I just couldn't visualize a dog called Lyndon, Richard, or Gerald working a grouse covert. Richard, of course, could be shortened to Dick, but can you imagine hollering that one into the darkness of an unfamiliar campground?

A third consideration for names were those ending in the letter "Y." I had known excellent dogs called Toby, Fanny, Curly, Misty, Buddy, and Katy, but once again, discretion was called for because dogs, like people, have a tendency to live up to their names. Call a dog Goofy, Dippy, or Windy, and you may end up with one epitomizing incompetence or flatulence. One of my high school chums, Jim Farrow, named his dog Digger, which he was until he excavated Mr. Many's prize azaleas. Thereafter, he was affectionately known as "Old Dead Digger."

Many dogs have been named after items of affection. One of my first was Sundy, who's namesake was a smelly Alaska crabbing vessel. As things turned out, I think the boat carried less odor than the dog. Sundy had a great nose for birds, but she also liked to roll in putrifying fish flesh; she could sniff out a carp carcass under two feet of dry loam. Later in life, my friend, Jim, had a little bitch chocolate Lab named after his mother–in–law. Snake–eyes was a pretty decent chukar dog, but when Jim started calling her "Snake," a lot of us stopped hunting with him. Snake had a tendency to range, and we got a little nervous when Jim yelled her name as we were clawing up a talus slope on all fours in rattler country.

So, where did all this insight, shared knowledge, and reflection take me? I wanted to call the last pup Mike. It was short, strong, and also the name of my favorite sports personality, Michael Jorbokowich, a local high school athlete who turned down a college basketball scholarship because the first practice fell on the pheasant opener. My wife, Lacey, who grew up in the suburbs of a large city, and who had not seen a dog larger than a wharf rat until she was out of high school, was partial to the names Muffin, Pookie, and Peaches—not exactly my ideal for a flushing dog who would earn his keep. My daughter, Jennifer, inspired no doubt by her careening hormones and the B+ she earned in a junior high Mythology class, preferred Adonis, and her brother, Matthew, was still solid on the name he had picked as a four–year–old: Fwinkster. Where that one came from is anyone's guess; the kid was strange at times.

Thank goodness for the American Kennel Club. We registered our pup as Adonis Fwinkster's Little Pookie and everyone is happy. I call him Mike.

The duck hunter workout

Every time a small supermarket here in town closes its doors to open a larger one a couple blocks away, the former sight is claimed immediately by a health spa charging exorbitant prices to make you sweat. Getting in shape has replaced self–awareness as the number–one priority of this decade, and paying to be miserable has become the "in" method of liberating your greenbacks. Personally, though, I think I'll stick to duck hunting where I can perspire and puff in the privacy of my own coveralls. It's not as trendy as weights and aerobics, but there's nothing like a flock of mallards to get my blood pumping, and if I want to look ridiculous in tights, I can always take off my clothes and hunt in my long underwear.

Men and women with only a modest knowledge of my sport are surprised, even suspicious, that I can lose 20 pounds each winter sitting in a duck blind. Judging by my overdrawn checks, always made out to "cash" to disguise various decoy and gasoline purchases, my own wife once suspected I was flying down to a private health clinic in Baja on weekends and paying professionals to knead and steam my summer flab into muscle. Not that I would ever win an Arnold Swartzenegger look–alike contest, but for a 50–year–old man who spends 60 hours a week at a desk, I don't look a day over 70. The truth is, 80% of all waterfowl hunting is spent outside the blind without a shotgun, and most of that time is monopolized by physical exertion that would make a triathalon seem like a marshmallow roast.

Putting out decoys is probably the best all–around exercise ever devised. To begin with, I must find my hip boots in the accumulated debris of what I call my "storage shed," but which is really an extra structure I built off the house to prevent fatalities when opening closets. Lacey complained so much about the avalanche of reloading supplies, shell vests, and water–carrying devices when she opened the closet door searching for the ironing board, I decided an out–structure for just my gear was the solution. Now, only I am inundated when the door is eased open. I burn a lot of calories just looking for things, and it doesn't seem to matter that I used them a week previously and carefully put them away. Alone in the dark of my storage shed, they slip quietly to the corners and bury themselves beneath tons of other hunting and fishing necessities.

There is also the problem of children. Mine have a phobia about putting anything back. If my son, for example, were to borrow the family refrigerator for a few hours, I might later find it in the driveway, under the boat, or in the weeds behind the raspberry bushes. Under no circumstances, however, would it be back in the kitchen where it belongs. Theoretically, locating the decoy sacks should not be all that difficult, for all I have to do is find the decoys and the sacks will be covering them. Ha! When my kids go off to a slumber party, or even their grandmother's, they would sooner perish than carry their clothes in one of the grey leather suitcases I bought for such occasions. No, they would much rather use one of my decoy sacks. "Duffel bags," they call them. "All the guys have one, Dad. Nobody uses suitcases anymore, Dad. We don't remember where we put them, Dad. Did you check the refrigerator?" Anyway, the swearing, the storming, the digging, and the 400 trips to the storage shed are always good for losing a few pounds and loosening up the old vertebrae. This is fortunate, too, as the back will get a real workout later on and it is best not to go into the marsh too tight. There is no way you can get into hip boots with a tight back.

I am not certain when the act of putting on a pair of hip boots attained its status as high comedy, but judging from the furtive snickers and outright guffaws of my hunting partners, it is better than a Jonathan Winters/Robin Williams armpit duet. I have explained almost tearfully that lower back spasms are hereditary in my family and extremely uncomfortable besides, but this does nothing to silence the callous merriment exhibited by both Mark and Mike as I sit on the tailgate of my truck and attempt to lasso my feet with my boots without bending over. Sometimes, this process is accomplished in as few as 10 minutes, but 18 is a good average, and 25 not uncommon—excellent for tightening stomach muscles and keeping the rotator cuff in shape, to say nothing of the massive deposits of ugly cholesterol flushed from my veins as I fume and thrash.

Eventually, after a long drive on an empty stomach, I am ready for the actual setting of the decoys, the only element of my duck hunting expeditions that Lacey says sounds fun at all. I have tried to explain figure eights and fish hooks to her, but I think she visualizes some grand orchestration, some artistic endeavor in which the hunter directs the creative placement of his blocks from a leather–backed swivel chair. It's more like a water ballet, I try to tell her, but the water is partially iced over, the slippers are full of mud, the lights are out, and the performers keep stumbling. Setting out five dozen mallard decoys on a dark December morning is as artistic as the stuff frozen in my mustache and about half as fun as a chapped butt. Still, it must be good for me because I ache terribly by the end of the day. After a season of such jollity, I can jerk a full hip boot of water out of the mud in less than two minutes, and though my thigh muscles don't exactly bulge while doing so, my eyes always do.

Finally in the blind, the duck hunter is now sweating profusely from his exertions, but it isn't long before he begins to shake. Poets of the Marsh, those outdoor writers who can take a common phrase and twist it until it sings, say these palpitations are caused by anticipation and primitive desire, and while there is truth to this, there is also the reality that it's darn cold. Often, after placing the decoys, the hunter is unable to keep the pond water in his boots at body temperature. Many people call the resulting phenomenon "the chills," but duck hunters call it "freezing your num–nums off." In any event, it burns a lot of calories.

Perhaps surprisingly, even sitting in the blind is not the sedentary activity one would imagine. Never has a waterfowl hunter lived who has constructed a blind that pleased him, and many hours are spent deleting and adding material to his place of concealment. Combine this tendency with bluebird weather and boredom, and his physical exertion becomes constant. My own favorite hunting blind is honeycombed with tunnels, shelves, and depressions, theoretically scooped out to store gear and make sitting more comfortable, but actually created solely to give me something to do while waiting for ducks that were slow to show up. My favorite spot in this weekend shelter is the sheer, earthen wall behind me where I have formed my initials in two–foot letters by pounding spent casings into the dirt with a teaspoon until only the brass is visible. It is my fantasy that a half million years from now when my blind is excavated, anthropologists will see this shrine and assign it some monumental, primitive–man significance. They'll never guess it was part of a personal health spa.

Retrieving is the next exercise in The Duck Hunter Workout. Most of us have dogs for this stage of the hunt, but many of these, like my own, are off chasing muskrats when a duck is finally downed, and some must be followed to make sure the retrieve does not culminate on the opposite shore in a profusion of drifting feathers. Either way, wading across a chest–deep pond in thigh–high boots burns a good 500 calories per trip. The animated sloshing as the water reaches the V of the legs accounts for half of these.

At day's end, decoys must be picked up and sacked, but first the anchor cords must be rewound, a process equivalent to attempting fine embroidery wearing ski mittens. With fingers that feel like frozen wieners, it is an onerous task, prolonging the ordeal far beyond the exhaustion stage. And this, as every physical fitness buff knows, is the time your workout does the

most good. "Wind decoy cords 'til it hurts and then wind some more" is what I always say. It's not profound, but it beats Emily Dickinson's, "There is no frigate like a book," which, I might add, was a bit of a surprise as I didn't think they used cuss words during Emily's day. The last time I heard "frigate" was a year ago when Mike drove his Subaru up to a blind and then buried it to mid–door. "Frigate," he said, after an hour of futile shoveling. "Let's put out the decoys."

Even after picking up, the duck hunter is still left with a couple very effective exercises for losing weight and developing calf, thigh, and buttocks muscles. I call one of these *Walking for gas.* I'm not talking here about removing myself for a short stroll so as not to offend others in the party. I'm talking about hiking several miles to purchase petroleum products from a pump. Because I possess common human quirks that make me think the further I can go on my last gallon of petrol, the better my overall mileage will be (and the less I pay for a gallon, the better person I am), I frequently participate in this body–building technique. It is usually practiced far from major metropolises, where proprietors of service stations have dinner with their families and then go to bed, and where, by the time I decide to pay the extra three cents per gallon for enough to get me home, it's too late. And should I stumble upon a station far from nowhere that is open after seven p.m., I can then combine *Walking for gas* with *Lugging it back*, which is good for the biceps and pectorals. Few people know that carrying a five–gallon can of unleaded for three miles is equivalent to pressing 200 pounds 50 times while riding a stationary bike.

As mentioned, duck hunting is a total fitness program, and when finally home, even the larynx receives a workout as I try to talk someone into cleaning birds for me. It's late. I'm wet, cold, and hungry. My body aches. To my way of thinking, children and spouse should be honored and delighted to welcome back the mighty hunter with hot toddy and slippers, gazing at him fondly as they pick and draw the bounty he has provided. You bet. My fingers are the fittest part of my body. Plucking ducks at midnight is great for the terminal digits.

The animosity factor

Had my childhood not been so conspicuously dogless, I'm certain my adult life would be less cluttered with canine vagrants. Reality in the form of 60–dollar–a–month dog food bills, however, cannot be ignored, and I long ago gave up pretending the two extra dogs on my front porch are just visiting. That a bird hunting man needs a bird hunting dog is inarguable; that he needs two is suspect; when he adds a third, he darn well better be able to convince his wife it is the reincarnation of her favorite uncle. Wives are extremely hostile about giving up Friday nights out just so their husbands can afford to make doggy additions to the compost pile.

Second and third hunting dogs brought into a marriage partnership by one party without complete and prior approval of the other party are at a distinct disadvantage: there is an animosity factor that doesn't necessarily have anything to do with the dog. A fundamental tenet of marriage—that of sharing in all things, including puppy procurement—has been violated. New, "other" dogs must therefore be not only cute, intelligent, and lovable, they must possess the social graces of an Emily Post and be fastidious to the point of obsession. Unfortunately, my wife, Lacey, thinks Little Dude, a most recent acquisition, is severely deficient in at least five areas. Fortunately, he was adopted by a man of sanguine disposition, and more importantly, he retrieved a duck for me when he was but four months old. It matters not that the phenomenon has not since been repeated; potential alone will assure him a place in my heart for another 10 or 12 years, and you can never tell when he might decide to retrieve another. In the meantime, I must justify his sometimes disreputable behavior in the yard, house, and neighborhood using an optimistic system of conduct evaluation my spouse calls C.R.A.P. (Canine Review and Pardon). This is how it works:

Little Dude wanders onto the front lawn and begins to dig a hole. My wife stands at the living room window glaring angrily as the turf disappears. Her lips are set in a tight, thin line I never saw during our courting days. It makes me wonder about the initial attraction. Still, I neither panic nor cower. Rather than hasten to stop his demented digging, I lean back against my vehicle, smile with satisfaction, and watch the dirt spray from the excavation as if witnessing the creation of the Eighth Wonder of the World. "Do you see that?" I ask Lacey when she can stand it no longer and has sprinted into the yard wielding a spatula like a club. "Now how do you suppose that little dog knew exactly where I wanted to plant a lilac bush for your birthday?"

"That's C.R.A.P.," she replies, but somewhat less hostilely than could be expected.

On another day, Little Dude gets the munchies and chews the seat off a bicycle. "That animal is uncanny!" I tell my wife at dinner. "Already he understands my intense loathing for contrived exercise." Lacey informs me the bike is hers. I offer to replace the seat with a more comfortable, more expensive model, but she says she would rather have the money. Then she reminds me that a good marriage maintenance plan requires much more than periodic bicycle seat replacement.

I tried for a long time to keep Dude kenneled, but I may as well have tried to padlock the wind. Without a doubt, there was a badger somewhere in the woodpile of his ancestry because he didn't just dig holes under the wire, he created caverns that caused the kennel posts to sag and the wire to go slack. The morning after his first night of incarceration, he was sitting happily on the porch, his nose wet with sand, his long, black tail chiming against the barbecue grill, my wife's flower pots strewn across the yard. "Isn't that something!" I told Lacey. "All that trouble digging out so he could be here to feast his eyes on your loveliness as you plucked the morning paper from the porch."

Lacey squinted out from beneath a mud pack, swatted at her disheveled mane, and stuck out her tongue. "That's C.R.A.P., too," she said. But she smiled when she said it.

To eliminate the digging problem, I began dropping chunks of firewood into Dude's excavations, but every morning they were pushed to the side of an ever–deepening pit, the kennel posts were leaning yet further, and Dude was on the porch waiting for Lacey, a night of destruction spread out proudly for her to see. When I figured half our winter fuel supply was below ground, I gave up and left him out at night. Dude showed his immeasurable gratitude by going next door and methodically bringing the neighbor's wood pile home with him, one log at a time. I suggested to Lacey that working together, Dude and I could make a killing in the firewood business, perhaps even earning enough to buy the new car she wanted. The way I figured it, I could cut nine or ten cords of tamarack and then sell it in the neighborhood six or seven times over, during the winter. She, of course, vetoed the plan saying that when they put me in jail, she could use *my* car.

Before long, Dude, seeing no future in the firewood business, began to branch out. In the next month, he brought home a pair of golf shoes, a dog dish full of kibble, a fifty–foot section of rubber garden hose, two lawn mower tires, a TV antenna, and a rolled turkey roast *still on the barbecue spit*! Though I displayed all but the roast and kibble conspicuously in the driveway for a week, none were claimed. I told Lacey that with one or two more just like Dude, we could hold a garage sale every week, and wasn't it thoughtful of him to think of the family as he scrounged around the neighborhood? Most dogs, I said, would bring home scarcely more than an old

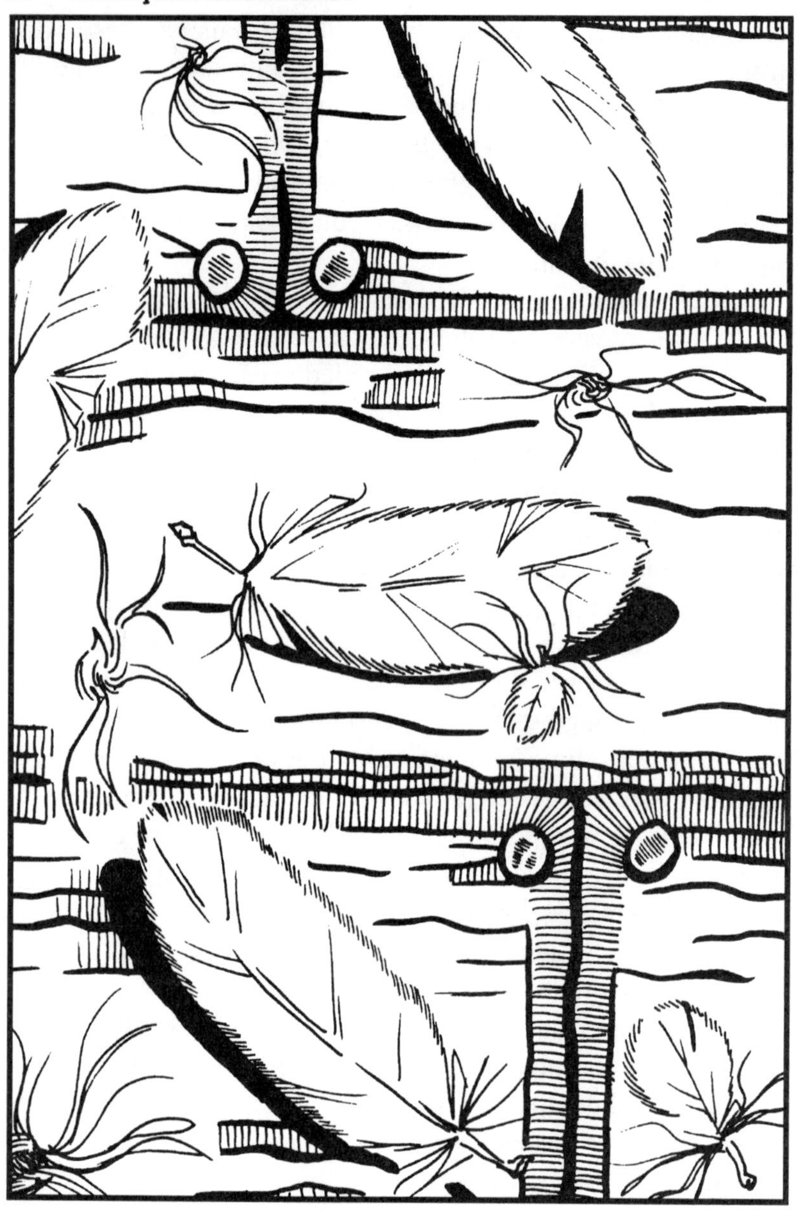

bone or TV dinner tray, selfishly excluding the hands that fed him. Lacey countered with a sarcastic statement about having to move closer to the county dump so we would have a place to store our newly–acquired "treasures." She mentioned C.R.A.P. that time, also.

Because he began to wander further in his quest for more exotic gifts, I soon decided we would have to keep Dude in the house at night. Lacey, of course, was dead–set against the idea until I convinced her to let us try just one time so she could see how indispensable he could be. Not only did Dude bark all night, thus keeping burglars from even *entering* the yard, the next morning when an entire carton of eggs was swept mysteriously from a counter top, he was there in an instant to lap them up before they could soak into the carpet. The next night, he began his "toilet paper inspection," unwinding an entire roll to check for defects. There was no way, I told Lacey, that she or I had time for this invaluable service. Nevertheless, Lacey now makes sure the bathroom doors are closed before coming to bed and locking the bedroom door. Sometimes if I'm not quick enough, Dude and I sleep together on the rug in front of the stove.

Last December, Lacey and I did all our Christmas shopping through mail order catalogues. The day the parcels were delivered, no one was at home, so Dude took it upon himself to open the packages himself and then carry them around for the neighbors to view. When I got home, Lacey was fit to be tied, but I told her we had luckily been spared the ordeal of attempting to rip and sort through yards of strapping tape and several tons of Styrofoam packing pellets. As things now stand, I told her, I have only to walk through the neighborhood gathering up the intended gifts. Conservatively, I said, it would save us two hours. Sure enough, I returned in a short time with every single item, but even so, Lacey complained that her Aunt Vi probably wouldn't like a down jacket with dog slobber where the pockets should be. Not so, I told her. The jacket was ever so much more chic with the streamlining—more C.R.A.P. to be sure, but I think I saw her smile.

It wasn't until late winter past that I learned my Canine Review and Pardon system worked two ways. A friend in Fairbanks had promised to send me a winter–plumage ptarmigan skin by overnight express. Naturally, Lacey wasn't too excited about me adding another mounted bird to my collection, and she complained loudly about the expense so soon after Christmas. The day the skin was to arrive, I hurried home from work and practically dove into the mailbox.

"If you're looking for your bird," Lacey called from the front porch, "it's in the back yard."

"What's it doing in the back yard?" I asked. "The dog will get it."

"Already has," Lacey said cheerfully.

White feathers. Nothing but white feathers. Drifting across the back porch, hanging from the woodpile, matted in soggy tufts on the muzzle of a black dog. "I'll destroy him!" I screamed. "I'll beat him to a pulp and then beat the pulp! I'll. . . ."

"Oh calm down, dear," Lacey said quietly. "You wouldn't hurt that dog and you know it. Obviously he heard me complain about the expense of another mounted bird, and to prevent marital discord—*further* marital discord, that is—he decided to eliminate the source of irritation."

"That's C.R.A.P.," I said meekly.

"That's right," Lacey replied.

Stachofsky's statutes

On a late October afternoon, Thayer Bogg and I were slogging through a cattail jungle, each burdened down with a mesh bag of duck decoys, our shotguns, and a two–quart thermos of coffee. Somewhere ahead, Thayer's dog, Darrell, and my Lab pup, Dude, enthusiastically explored the mucky tangles.

"Get a move on, brother–in–law," Thayer grunted from behind, "or them mallards will be fed, watered, and tucked in for the night before we even set up." He chuckled foolishly between gasps. "You got rocks in your pockets, or what?"

As a matter of fact, I *did* have rocks in my pockets—two handfuls to be exact, and the extra weight was bogging me down. No sense, though, trying to explain something as germane as Stachofsky's Statutes to a man who had once used a linoleum knife to purposefully put an L–shaped rip in his new hunting coat "So's I don't have to worry about it later," and I merely bit my tongue, gritted my teeth, and stumbled on, my mouth hurting like crazy.

Morton Stachofsky is Murphy Stachofsky's brother. Now, everyone is familiar with Murphy's Law, which states that whenever something can go wrong, it will. Well, Morton was more than a little jealous of all the attention Murphy was getting, so being a waterfowl hunter, he refined and elaborated on the basic law, making up a whole list of "go–wrongs" just for duck and goose gunners. So far, Morton hasn't gained the recognition of brother Murphy, and he probably never will because he went a little haywire a couple seasons back and they locked him up for setting out dove decoys in the Northgate Shopping Mall and attempting to terminate a flock of common pigeons with a blow gun.

Anyway, from Morton I got the idea of carrying rocks on my duck hunts. His first statute, in fact, was Throwin' Rocks Are Never There When You Need Them. Morton, like myself, had once experienced the hair–tearing frustration of knocking a duck stone dead in deep water and watching helplessly as his young dog swam by and around it. With just one small pebble, Morton could have directed the pup to his quarry with a gentle splash, but he was in the middle of a swamp and the closest rock was two miles away. In the same situation, I have tried throwing mud balls which just disintegrated in flight and cattail catkins which the dog retrieved. In desperation, I started chucking my #2 steel shot, and when the shell loops were empty, forfeited a can of butterscotch pudding, and finally, my right boot.

With frequent experiences like this one, it is no wonder Morton's elevator finally stopped between floors, but fortunately his Statutes were published in an obscure waterfowl hunter's journal, Pinheads and Pintails, before the men with the white coats came to take him away. With permission of the publisher, I have here reproduced some of Morton Stachofsky's Statutes, and for clarification have added a few elaborations of my own.

Pond water is always 1/4-inch deeper than your hip boots

Most duck hunters already know hip boots are merely rubber devices used for bringing pond water to body temperature, but still, they try to prolong the process. I, on the other hand, immediately fill my boots before entering the water because I have this theory that if I make enough trips back to shore to dump them, the pond will become shallower and my hunt will be more enjoyable the next time. Unfortunately, this excellent rationalization is frequently counteracted by another

Stachofsky Statute that states The shallower the water, the deeper the mud. Then, of course, there's The shorter your anchor cords, the deeper the water, and The colder the water, the less likely your patches will hold, but that's enough about H_20. Morton had plenty of others.

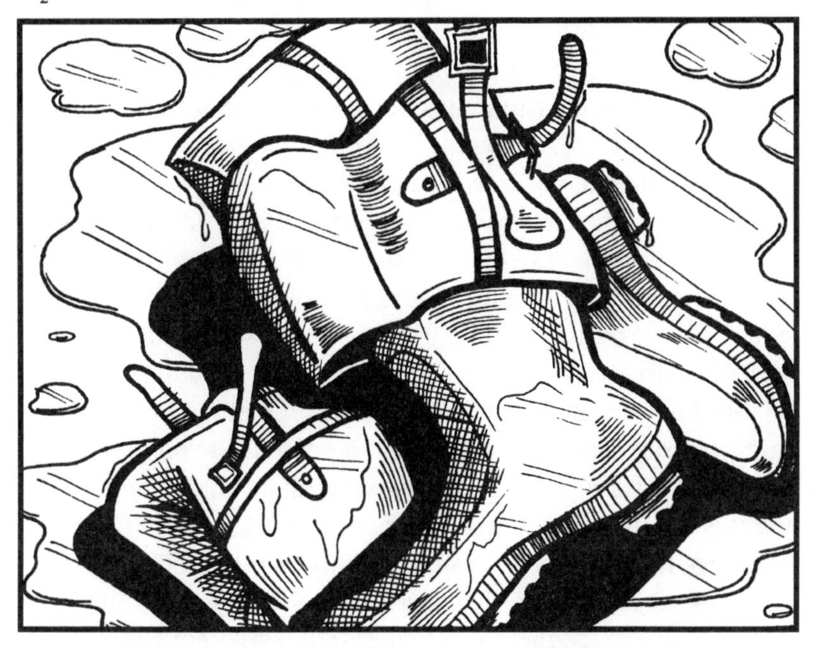

The fewer the ducks, the worse you'll shoot.

A couple of years back, a friend took me to his father's place an hour and a half south of town. We got up at 3 A.M., left at 3:30, drove through heavy fog, set out six dozen decoys, were in the blind by 6:30, and had two limits of mallards eight minutes later. Now don't get me wrong—I'm not complaining. I need a day like that every now and again to confirm the existence of a Greater Being who watches over small boys, young dogs, and old duck hunters. The thing is, though, we then hung around the blind a couple more hours taking pictures of thousands of ducks, all of which wanted to land only on our pond. Had I not gone four for four, I could have enjoyed the smell of gun powder all day. Contrast that trip with a more typical one during which I sit all day in a frozen blind for shots at three singles, all of which are missed. It isn't fair.

The larger the area, the more likely you'll have to share it.

Waterfowl and waterfowl hunters are a gregarious bunch, but most hunters would agree their sport is more fun if the nearest competitor is not sitting in their lap. It is uncanny how often a novice gunner on big water will try to set out blocks within a few yards of those of another party. Probably, this is because of an insecurity intensified by loneliness, but I suspect it also involves a certain amount of brain damage. These same people are the ones who will enter a near–empty bus, walk all the way down the aisle to the back, and squeeze in next to the only other passenger, which is usually me. There are, of course, methods of dealing with these dolts, but they aren't all legal. The bus driver will help, but sometimes it is difficult to find a bus driver in a duck marsh.

My favorite, and by far most effective, method of discouraging encroachers in my swamp is to put a decoy on my head and squat–walk past their blind talking like Donald Duck. The effect is compounded immeasurably when I fall over on my side from time to time and thrash wildly in place like a wind–up toy gone gunnysack. If this doesn't discourage the interloper, I will engage them in a conversation wherein I mention that my hunting partner is subject to violent, unprovoked attacks, and why they ever let him out is beyond me.

The more distant the spot, the worse the roads.

I am fortunate to live in an area that offers a variety of waterfowl hunting experiences within 30 miles of my front door, but I often opt for a longer drive just for a change of scenery. A good part of hunting is, after all, just getting out and seeing some new areas and bolstering their economy through the purchase of gasoline, food, and tow truck services.

There is a constant in driving to my duck and goose spots that, if charted, would clearly show a direct relationship between distance and nastiness of roads and weather. Any drive under 30 miles, for example, will always be on a new four–lane with optimum visibility. Over a hundred miles, and I can count on fog, black ice, frost heaves, freezing rain, and a porcupine in the middle of the road every eight minutes. Over 150 miles and I'll find all of the above plus drunk drivers and downed power lines.

The more you brag about it, the worse it will be.

There is probably nothing I like more than to sit at the edge of a circle of friends, smiling astutely, sucking thoughtfully on a pipe and indulging in quiet condescension while they rave about a duck or goose hunting spot they've discovered. This is not accomplished without difficulty as I don't smoke any more, but knowing *my* spot has theirs beat hands down makes the effort worthwhile. "Hey," one of them will eventually ask, looking at me suspiciously, "how come *you're* not saying anything?" That, of course, is the moment I have been waiting for.

"Shoot," I'll say, feigning boredom, "you guys don't know what really good bird hunting is all about." Then, after several minutes of intense interrogation, I'll reluctantly let them weasel into my confidence. Pretty soon one of them will offer to drive, another to pack my lunch, and a third to load me up a couple boxes of shells if I'll take them to my secret spot.

In truth, I sometimes *do* locate a winter wheat field where the honkers are determined to land no matter how inadequate my camouflage, or a hidden slough where mallards and pintails set their wings 200 yards away and come in without circling. When I take others back with me, however, the place has become a dead zone—not even a feather to indicate waterfowl had ever been in the area. "I can't figure it out," I'll say, trying to avoid their hateful glares. "Last week I couldn't keep them out of the decoys." Then, I eat as much lunch as quickly as possible before the sorrowful truth sinks completely in, and try to beat the others to the car when they've called it a day. On the way to town, scrunched between decoy sacks, ignored by even the dogs, I remember another Stachofsky Statute: <u>The more disappointing the hunt, the longer the drive home</u>.

The coyote reflex

There is nothing like waiting three hours in a doctor's reception room with a single, worn, 12–year–old U.S. News and World Report to make one question the necessity of a check–up. Still, I *had* been feeling listless again. Except for a few years at college where I had burned the candle at both ends *and* the middle, I had always taken pretty good care of my body, and it disturbed me to admit that the last few hunting seasons I had returned from my days afield with barely enough energy to shuck my boots.

Just when I had decided the doctor was hiding in the back room, peeking through a crack, and giggling at how long he could keep 40 people crammed into his small waiting room, a corpulent woman in a white uniform and silly little hat called my name, shoved me into a stark cubicle, and told me to disrobe. "The doctor will be with you shortly," she growled, shoving half a dressing gown at me. "Put this on."

I spent nearly 20 minutes trying to decide whether to cover my front or my rear with the fragmented garment, but once I had made the choice, there was nothing to do but sit there on the crinkly piece of paper covering the examination table and wonder what I would do if there was a fire. Then, beneath a jar of cotton balls, I spotted one of those informative, boring pamphlets written by the medical profession who consider them high entertainment. It was entitled "Everything You Didn't Want to Know About the Adrenal But We're Telling You Anyway."

Skimming listlessly through my reading material, trying not to feel ridiculous with my dressing gown hanging like a Batman cape down my back, and feeling rather chilled, I killed time waiting for a doctor who, as far as I knew, was off somewhere playing golf and thinking of other humiliating things to make his patients wear. Under the circumstances, I would have much preferred reading something on justifiable homicide or creative head–butting, but I sat there with the thing anyway, and pretty soon was completely absorbed by the fascinating world of suprarenal secretions.

Adrenaline, it seems, is a natural hormone secreted by the body in times of anxiety and excitement. It contracts the blood vessels and speeds heart action, thus giving an individual a temporary power surge which allows him to attempt to overcome his particular trauma. Afterwards, the pamphlet said, there is a let–down as the body recovers from the additional exertion.

So there it was—the reason for the tiredness I experienced after a day of hunting. I wasn't sick, I was suffering from the normal after–effects of *The Coyote Reflex.*

In the animal world, any specie of the canine persuasion at one time ran with a pack. Dogs did, wolves and coyotes still do. When the pack is hunting, it is imprudent for a member to stumble, as the others, with no particular concern about friendship or relationship, and no noticeable remorse, will turn on him as he goes down. If his adrenals are not working right and he cannot quickly recover, the hunt will end at this point; the unfortunate becomes dinner. And so it is in my circle of hunting acquaintances. Though they will "eat me alive" only in the figurative sense if I stumble, the output of adrenalin is no less.

My coordination and luck being what they are, I am perpetually attracted to sink holes, unstable outcroppings, and pools of duckweed–covered water that appear to be a few inches deep but are over my head. My hunting acquaintances being what *they* are, are inclined to laugh mercilessly when I find one of these. It is therefore necessary that on a typical hunt I call forth tremendous amounts of adrenalin in freeing myself and becoming upright again before my predicament is noted. If I don't, I will be consumed by the base sarcasm of my "friends." "Been walking long?" and "See anything interesting down there?" are two of their favorite digs, followed by riotous laughter and animated, exaggerated re–creations of my disconcertion. Though not life–threatening, I would as soon not go through it more times than absolutely necessary. Creeping age and ten miles a day had nothing to do with my tiredness; my body was forever recovering from adrenalin expenditure.

My self diagnosis complete, I stepped down from the examination table and removed the dressing gown just as the nurse popped her head in the room. "The doctor will be with you in. . . . Oh my! You *do* look bad," she giggled.

Quickly wrapping the obnoxious half–garment around my hips like a diaper, I threw myself against the door. The Coyote Reflex. I could feel my heartbeat double. No doubt I'd be exhausted again when I made my exit, but I smiled anyway as I got dressed. I figured the nurse would be having an adrenalin rush of her own because that silly little hat of hers had been slammed in the door.

The Eleventh Commandment

Way back when kids read because they wanted to and you could still find a hero in major league baseball, my favorite comic strip was called, simply, "Nancy." Nancy had a friend (boyfriend, steady, significant other?) called Sluggo, and what I remember most about them now is how they never did anything rude, crude, or socially unacceptable. Often, they went fishing, but seldom did they catch any fish. With high expectations, Sluggo would drop his line from a public dock and then reel in an old boot, an inner tube, or a tin can. I, of course, found this wildly hilarious, but bear in mind that my idea of high entertainment was picking cheat grass from my socks or frying ants on the sidewalk with a magnifying glass. Bear in mind, also, that my idea of environmental awareness was knowing what time the nightcrawlers came out on Kostelecky's lawn.

Today, the litter problem on lakes and rivers is anything but funny, and I have read of bodies of water into which old tires and bed springs had been intentionally and *legally* dumped to create fish habitat. While this may be considered aggressive and creative fish management by some, I'm old fashioned and would rather entice my fish from kelp beds, natural reefs, and undercuts than a 7.50–16 whitewall. Also, I have enough problems with snags on sandy bottoms and can't imagine what would happen were I to fish in an underwater jungle of rusted

bed springs. With my luck, I'd land one and someone from the local paper would be there to take my picture.

For many years now, I have carried on a zealous program for cleaning up local waters. Usually, I try to be civil about the whole thing, but sometimes civil is not effective. If this is the case, I am capable of conducting my anti–litter campaign with as much subtleness as a bad case of diarrhea, confronting and berating slob boaters and fishermen about their "out of sight, out of mind" mentality. I find it appalling that a person who would not dream of dropping a pop or beer can in his own driveway will dispose of his empties overboard in my lake, and my lambasting is spiced with a whole bunch of words like "tatterdemalion, dotard," and "soporific." If my Aunt Doreen's along, we make numerous references to genealogy, anatomy, and sexual persuasions; Aunt Doreen has a bigger vocabulary than I, and she likes litterers even less.

There are, of course, softer ways of making the same point, but an individual must adapt his method of rebuke to his own personality and level of frustration. A friend of mine, Riley Shook, eases his boat alongside the offenders, scoops up their bobbing litter in his landing net, and deposits it from whence it came. "You lost this," he says, rising to his full 6' 9" and smiling sweetly.

Another friend, Steve Pope, is more ingenious, and of us all, probably makes the greatest impression. Boldly nosing his inboard against the bow of the litterer's craft, he stands up, briefly but dramatically flashes a gold–embossed credit card, and announces his affiliation with the N.L.C.—Nautical Litter Control.

"Mornin' folks," he drawls, camouflaging his Yankee heritage. Steve has a theory that everyone is familiar with the odious lawman in the movie, Cool–Hand Luke, and is terrified by a man of authority with a Dixie accent. "Seems we got us a problem here." Then he removes his sunglasses, wipes his forehead with a forearm, shakes his head, and sighs a troubled sigh as he smacks his fish billy against the palm of one hand. The occupants of the boat, uncertain of just what it is they are dealing with, watch timidly as Steve rests one boot on their bow and takes a note pad from his back pocket. They don't know it's his fishing diary.

"What's the problem, sir?" they invariably ask.

Steve glares at them, seems to tremble, then points a finger at the litter in the water. "Don't argue!" he snarls. Then, he wipes the heel of his palms on the sides of his trousers as if to regain composure. "What we got here," he begins again, "is a lack of com–munication." He pauses, searching each face accusingly. "You folks," he continues, "are in di–rect vi–o–lation of Co–mandment eleven dash B which is *clearly* posted at the launch and which *clearly* communicates the message, 'Thou shalt not dee–posit unnatural, man–made sub–stan–ces in this here waterway'."

The boaters/fishermen look guiltily at one another.

"Now," Steve says, "accordin' to the law of this here great state, y'all either clean up yer own mess, plus an hour policin' the boat ramp fer cigarette butts an' such, or me'n Bubba will hafta pull y'all in." He jerks a thumb in my direction and I stand, uncoiling the tow rope. Proof of the effectiveness of Steve's ploy is the fact that never in 12 years has he had to tow anyone to shore, and never has he encountered a repeat violator. The boat ramp is spotless.

As much as I despise litter, there have been a few times it has made me smile. One of those was on Loon Lake where I was dangling a jig in deep water off the dock hoping to entice a large, but rather aloof mackinaw known to prowl the vicinity. Inadvertently, my jig dropped into the top of a rusted, partially–opened tin can, and when I "landed" it, I was pleased to find a crawdad inside. Adding it to my jig, I resumed fishing. Sure enough, I *still* didn't catch that mack, but it would have made such a good story, I told everyone I did.

Another time, I was jigging deep water for walleye in the Columbia River when I had a tremendous strike. The fish was powerful, and every time I got it off the bottom, it would shake its head and dive again. Following a half–hour, see–saw battle during which I attracted the Coast Guard and quite a number of charter boats with my enthusiastic whoops, I brought the monster to gaff. After all the hullabaloo, my wife insisted I bring it home for mounting, and I did, too. Today it hangs proudly in my garage, gray with age and a little warped—all eight feet of it. I had no idea a sheet of plywood could be so much fun.

Dear Cousin Judy:

When I told Lacey I owed you a letter, she quoted me some guy called St. Bernard who supposedly once said something about hell being full of good intentions. Tell me, cuz—how much credibility can you give a fellow who has been dead eight hundred and some years and was named after a big dog? If people were to start wrapping their lives around quotations of dead men, I'm sure they could find either justification or damnation for everything they do or don't do. A man named Peter Abellard, for instance, once said, "Against the disease of writing one must take special precautions." And that is why this letter is so long in coming.

If you must know, the real reason my correspondence is so erratic is because my work days are getting longer, my weekends shorter, and my New Years Eves closer together. Essentially, those special hours I call my "livin' time" seem to have been cut in half, and it's hard to sit at home writing letters when the bass are taking top–waters or the ducks are flying. Fortunately, there are times such as today, when rain is falling in buckets and memories of the hunting and fishing seasons are no more than occasional spasms in the vicinity of my wallet. On days like this, Judy, I have an uncontrollable desire to type a letter and prove my high school typing teacher, Miss Homerow, made a hasty evaluation when she told me I would never know my asterisk from my space bar.

It seems just yesterday that Georgie, Bonnie Rae, and I were plucking mallards on your front lawn. Those are two fine kids you and George are raising there, cousin. No, I never did get all the little feathers off the wool pants, and I apologize again for wearing them at the dinner table. Perhaps it's a good thing you discovered the allergy when you did, though. I knew a man whose wife bought him a goose down vest, and every time he put it on, his throat swelled shut. By the time he finally figured out the real source of irritation, he had torn out all the carpet in his home, given away two cats, and sold his dog. Then, his wife got disgusted and ran off to her sister's in Seattle. He says he misses the dog a lot.

I am flattered you want my recipe for fried mallard, but I still feel waterfowl is better plucked and baked, and I only served it fried that one time because of an unusual set of circumstances. In all due respect to your culinary expertise, I think one or two of these steps can be omitted, but per your request, I have left nothing out:

Fried Duck Ingredients:
Two mallard drakes, 1/2 cup flour, 1 tsp salt, 1/2 tsp pepper, 1/2 lemon, 1 black Lab, 1/2 cup orange juice, 2 Tbls cooking oil.

To begin with, Judy, I got those mallards while jump–shooting Rock Creek on a Saturday. I don't know if that had anything to do with the flavor and tenderness or not; it's possible that Sunday ducks over decoys would be even better. These were feeding on duck weed prior to the flush, but their crops were full of wheat—winter soft white, I think. It was late afternoon and the temperature was a –17 degrees with a north wind at 24 mph and just a hint of snow. By the time I got them home, they were frozen solid, so I hung them in the wood shed with plans to do the plucking on Sunday. As luck would have it, however, Dick Maroney called and invited me to go steelhead fishing, so I didn't get around to it that day, either. Well, making a living got in the way again, one thing led to another, the weather didn't improve, and it was two weeks before I got those poor ducks into the house to thaw. They lay in my kitchen sink approximately six hours, but then Dick called again, so I took them back to the wood shed where they hung another three days. At the time, they were half–thawed, but they quickly re–froze.

Finally, guilt got the better of me, I turned down a goose hunting trip, stayed home, and got those birds ready to pick. As you can imagine, their feathers did not come off the way they do on a fresh kill. In frustration, I skinned them, removed the legs, and filleted the meat off the breast bone. That, I placed in the refrigerator, intending to cook it for dinner, but Lacey's sister invited us over for chili dogs, I had night school the next evening, and then I plumb forgot them until you guys showed up.

Okay—here, I think, is the really important part: when I took the filleted breasts and legs from the refrigerator, I set them on the counter to bring to room temperature. Dude, that big, black Lab of mine, came by, reared up on his hind feet, and slurped up the whole bowlful. Naturally, I yelled when I saw him, and he spit out all but one little leg. I washed off what I had reclaimed, rolled it in the seasoned flour, and fried it three minutes per side in cooking oil over a medium flame. Then, I added the juice and grated peel of the lemon to the orange juice, poured it over the fillets, and simmered 20 minutes.

Like I said, I imagine one or two of these steps can be altered or even omitted, but you said *everything* was important so that's what I have given you. Personally, I don't think the lemon juice made a bit of difference, and you might want to go with less salt.

Let me know how it comes out. You can use Dude if you want, but I think your golden retriever will do just fine.

See ya in October!

Alan

You just gotta ask

I think what I like both least and most about women is they don't know the rules. Mostly, their actions are based on instinct; they can love and hate and laugh and cry without analysis, without guilt, and without reason, and when they have something to say, they say it. If you doubt any of this, you have never been fishing with my Aunt Doreen.

Until last Saturday, I hadn't been fishing with my Aunt Doreen, either. Mainly, that was because Aunt Doreen didn't fish. When she materialized on my doorstep, though, purple–white hair blowing every which way, she announced she thought it high time we "wet a line together."

"Since when are you into fishing?" I asked. All the relatives knew that at 73 years of age, Aunt Doreen's interests had begun to lean away from crocheting and more towards rejuvenating Milton, her 82–year–old boy friend. But we didn't suspect she had begun fishing.

"Since two days ago, you piscatorial person you," Aunt Doreen quipped, stepping into the house. "The postman brought me a copy of The Outdoor Press and I've been reading up. Seems the silvers are socking streamers off of Steamboat Rock, walleye are whopping worms on the Kettle, and big browns are bushwhacking black Rapalas in Rock Lake." She grinned up at me, obviously pleased with her newly–acquired angling terminology. "And this old gal wants her nephew to take her fishin'."

"Suits me fine, Aunt Doreen," I said. "I didn't even know you subscribed to The Outdoor Press."

"I don't," she whispered, looking warily around, "but the postman's new, and he doesn't know that. It's suppose to be going into Bill Wagstaff's box next door."

"Well, that's nice," I said, "and it so happens I was about to call Bill to see if he wanted to harass the bass right here in Loon Lake this afternoon. Let's you and I do it instead." Aunt Doreen brightened and I was pleased. It had been years since I'd introduced a novice to fishing.

We backed my boat out of the slip and headed toward the best bass habitat on the northeast side of the lake. In the first bay, two fishermen in a rubber raft were casting the shoreline and I cut the engine as we approached. "Doin' any good?" I called.

"Some," one of them replied after a delay.

"Any size?" I called again.

"Not bad," he said.

"Top water?" I asked as we bobbed closer.

"Too cold for top water," he shrugged without looking up.

"Well, good luck," I said, waving as we backed away.

Aunt Doreen was looking at me curiously. "And just what was that all about?" she asked.

"What?"

"That nonsense that just took place over there," she said, jerking her thumb toward the other fishermen. "If you didn't want an answer, why did you bother to ask questions?" She studied me curiously. "You don't know any more now than you did when we first got here."

I shrugged weakly, cranked up the outboard, and pointed the boat down the lake. "It's part of fishing," I said.

At the next bay, which was also occupied, I repeated my questions for a single fisherman in a fiberglass tri–hull while Aunt Doreen fidgeted in the bow. His answers were similarly evasive.

"You did it again," Aunt Doreen accused when we pulled away. "Now lookee here, Nephew, I didn't come fishin' to swat mosquitoes and listen to you play the fool. There wasn't anything in The Outdoor Press that said I'd have to sit through such nonsense. I'm wanting to hang me a halibut, and we haven't even put our lines in the water."

"We're after bass, Aunt Doreen," I corrected. "There are no halibut in fresh water."

"As far as I know, there aren't any bass, either," she said, scorching me with a look. "Now tell me something, Nephew—you didn't just bring your old Aunt Doreen out here to humor her, did you? Criminy, boy, I've been on boat rides. You said we were going fishin'."

"We are, we are," I promised, "but it's like this: you don't just waltz up to another fisherman and ask him flat out to show you his fish and what he caught them on. What I'm doing here is prospecting. It's a process designed to eventually save time. The trick is to get them talking and then slip in a few trick questions. Pretty soon, you have some clues. Then, you put the clues together, and before you know it, you have all the information you need."

"Like with those other guys?" Aunt Doreen smirked.

"Well, I must admit, they were a trifle grumpy," I said, "but sooner or later, someone will mess up. Trust me—it's faster than experimenting." I looked at her for a nod of understanding, but she was still shaking her head.

"Sounds like male nonsense to me," she grumbled, "but tell me more. I want to do this fishin' thing right."

"The main thing," I said with a little more confidence, "is not to let on you're really all that interested. Most times, you start with a 'How's the fishin'?' and then ease into questions about lures and presentation. It's important—especially here. Very few people know how to fish Loon Lake for bass, and those who do are tight–lipped."

Aunt Doreen cocked her head and squinted across the water. "It's a game, isn't it? One of those guy–things." Before I could reply, she continued. "But we're partners on this expedition, aren't we?"

"Yes ma'am. We're partners."

"So it seems to me you've been doing all the work."

"Well, I. . . ."

"So now I guess it's my turn," she said.

"That's fine," I replied, "but I really don't mind. We could just start casting, I guess. There's a trick to asking, you know. You have to catch them off guard."

Aunt Doreen pursed her lips. "My specialty," she stated. "I corraled your Uncle Benjamin, didn't I?" She shaded her eyes and searched the big bay in front of us. "Pull in next to that boat down by the island."

In a couple minutes, I shut down the motor, coasted through a patch of dollar pads, and stopped 30 feet from a middle–aged man working the shore–line from his 12–footer. Immediately, Aunt Doreen was standing. "Howdy," she called.

The man looked at her over his shoulder, continued reeling, and swung his lure quickly into the boat. "Howdy," he said at last. I remember thinking he was going to be a tough one.

"Didja feed the dog this morning?" Aunt Doreen called.

The fisherman looked up and stared blankly. "You talking to me?" he finally asked.

"'Course I'm talkin' to you," Aunt Doreen called back. "Ya take sugar in yer coffee or ya drink it black?"

"Huh?"

"Didja hug yer kids and toe the mark? Does yer underwear bind?"

"Lady, I don't. . . ." The man laid his fishing rod across the boat seats and shifted around to face us.

"Can you see the forest for the trees? Can ya win fer losin'? Do ya ever go without saying?"

"Lady. . . ." He looked at me pleadingly and reached for a cigarette, tearing at the package like a child with a Christmas present.

Aunt Doreen sat down and smiled. "How'm I doing?" she inquired. "Is that enough questions?"

"Whatever you think, Auntie," I said meekly. Hunched over a seat, I was trying to be inconspicuous.

Aunt Doreen grinned, turning back to the tormented fisherman. "Hey mister!" she called. "Hold up your fish so we can see 'em." Without hesitation, he did. "Those are real pretty," she beamed. "Whatcha usin'?"

Numbly, the man held up his fishing rod and dangled the lure above the water. "Chartreuse spinner bait," he mumbled. "Cast right into shore and then reel like crazy. If they don't take it right off, finish up kinda slow." He had managed to bring a cigarette to his mouth and was trying to light it with a tube of sun screen. Most of the tobacco was crumbled on his tee–shirt.

"Why, thank you kindly," Aunt Doreen called. "And now, would you mind movin' over a tad so we can have some room?"

Without reply, the man fumbled with the starter cord, keeping an eye on us the entire time. The engine caught and he twisted the throttle wide open. In seconds, the boat was on plane, skipping through the pads.

Aunt Doreen waved as he turned out of the bay and headed up the lake towards Granite Point Resort. Then, she relaxed and flipped open my tackle box. "Now wasn't that better?" she asked, rummaging through the trays. "You men make everything so difficult. All you gotta do is ask."

B. S. records

Following our last family get–together, my brother–in–law, Thayer Bogg, cornered me in the kitchen where I was enjoying a quiet cup of coffee. "Didja hear about my record blue grouse?" he asked seriously, pulling up a chair.

"Why no," I said automatically, before processing the statement. "Boone and Crockett?"

"Bogg and Snibble," Thayer replied. "Me and Ramsey next door started our own set of records for game birds. Figured someone ought to do it. We call it B and S Records."

"No doubt there is a need," I said, still only vaguely aware of what I was saying and wishing I had opted to go to bed early.

Thayer pulled a toothpick from his shirt pocket and leaned back in his chair. "Glad you approve," he smiled, "because to make the organization official, we elected officers, and you've been elected secretary and treasurer."

"How wonderful!" I said sarcastically. "A majority vote, no doubt."

"Well, almost," Thayer said seriously. "Ramsey voted for me, but I don't have a computer and you do, so I talked him into changin' his vote."

"I'm flattered, Thayer," I said, "I really am, but how did I get mixed up in this?"

Thayer dug furiously at a back molar with the toothpick. "Like I said, we needed a computer and you're the only one we know who's got one. And as for treasurer, we figured, 'aw what the heck.' You're a good guy, and mostly honest, too, though somewhat tight when it comes to. . . ." He paused. "Besides, there aint no money to handle—just a few supplies."

"What kind of supplies?"

"Measurin' stuff," Thayer said. "Post office scales, a cloth tape, pencils, and a tablet. And you better come on over and pick them up real soon 'cause as secretary, you'll be responsible for measurin' and recordin'."

"I am truly honored, Thayer," I said with more lost sarcasm. "And how does the Bogg and Snibble system work?" Despite a previous resolve to never again get involved in one of Thayer's screwball schemes, it seemed I was, and each time it was the same: I started by just barely sticking my toe in the water, and pretty soon I was soaking wet and thrashing around up to my eyeballs.

Thayer let the chair down easy. "Well, last year it was pretty simple," he said. "We just went by weight. But this year we want to be more official. You'll take the length of the longest feather in the tail and add it to body weight. Then. . . ."

"Hold it, hold it, hold it," I said, waving my hands as if to erase his words. "Ounces and inches can't be combined. You can't add length to weight."

"Well, I know *I* can't," Thayer said with some impatience, "but that's why you're secretary. Ya shoulda never run for secretary if ya didn't think ya could do the job. Now let me finish, will ya?"

I nodded, grimacing.

"Then," Thayer continued, "you take the circumference of the thigh, multiply that by the distance between the eyes, and add them together. Then. . . .Why you shakin' your head, brother–in–law?"

"It's no good, Thayer," I said. "It won't work."

"Even if we divide by the wing span?" he said hopefully.

Thayer looked so crestfallen, I was immediately sorry I had to throw a monkey wrench into his ambitious formula. He wasn't the greatest scholar in the world, but he was a decent husband to my sister, and what he lacked in gray matter he often compensated for with enthusiasm. It was obvious now that this record thing meant a lot to him. "Errrr. . .ahhhh. . ." I searched for words to restore his smile. "The paper work will be insurmountable," I finally said. "This BS system of yours will be so popular with bird hunters they'll want you to establish shot–size records, gauge records, probably even shot–size by gauge records. You've seen how it is with fishing, haven't you? Line class, rod class, fresh water, salt water, men's division, women's division, men with beards, women with pierced ears, men with pierced ears who know women with beards. . . ."

"Okay, okay, I get the picture." Thayer scratched his chin thoughtfully. "It would be a hassle," he admitted. "I saw in the paper the other day that a guy over in Cusick set a line class record catchin' an eight–ounce brookie on 30–pound line."

"That's right," I said, "and next week someone will establish another record with an eight–ouncer on 70–pound test. Tell you what, Thayer. . ."

"What?"

"Let's you and I and Ramsey Snibble put 20 bucks each in a pot, and whoever comes up with the pheasant with the longest tail feather takes it all. Maybe that way one of us can afford to have a bird mounted."

Thayer agreed enthusiastically. I didn't see any need to tell him I already had a 23–incher in the freezer.

Fun ticket toms

No doubt, the bad luck started a long time before the rain. It even started before I missed my shot at the big, strutting, blue–headed gobbler. Perhaps the bad luck began while I waited irritably for my luggage in the Medford, Oregon airport and my luggage waited for me in Portland, but more likely, it began back home, where five days earlier I had been reading the obituaries and brooding over an impending birthday. A fellow I'd gone to school with had keeled over and died while doing pushups on his front lawn. "That could have been you," an inner voice warned me. "Take a hike!" I said defiantly. An inner voice, especially, should have known I don't do pushups, and no one would be benevolent enough to call the patch of greenish–yellow vegetation in front of my house a lawn.

"What did you say, dear?" my wife called from the kitchen.

"I need to embrace life," I told her impetuously, "to use up my fun tickets while the roller coaster's still running. I'm going to call that turkey guide in Medford, Oregon—the one that found a gobbler for Herb last April."

Lacey entered the living room wiping her hands on her apron. I could smell her world–famous German chocolate cake in the oven. "I spent a summer in Oregon when I was a kid," she said. "The southern half—not too far from Medford. It's beautiful. But couldn't you embrace life a little closer to home? Maybe we could use up a fun ticket or two this Friday night at Milford's Oyster Bar."

"It's not just turkey hunting," I told her. "It's got to do with my 'three score and ten.' Life is short and getting shorter, and I want to do some things I've never done."

"Same here," Lacey said with a sigh. "As a matter of fact, I've been considering embracing life, too. In Paris. I've never been to France, you know. It's got to do with *my* three score and ten which is the balance on my Master Card. The bank gets nervous when my balance gets so low."

"Can you afford to go to Paris?" I asked, somewhat unnerved.

"Can you afford to go to Oregon?" she countered.

"No," I said, thumping my hand on the obituary column on the coffee table, "but *this* guy could and he didn't, and now he can't. When it's time to put me in the ground, I want to have just enough money in my pocket for the parking meter outside the funeral home."

That same afternoon I made hunting arrangements with John Lehnherr, reputed to be one of the best turkey guides in southern Oregon. And though Lacey didn't go to France, she did go shopping—Lamonts, Nordstroms, the Bon Marche, and the Emporium. Before I left, the Master Card people were breathing easy again.

The man at the airport claims counter was congenial as he searched the computer for my missing luggage. When he confirmed its loss, he gave me a small plastic packet containing a toothbrush and paste, a razor, some soap, and a small container of shampoo. "There you are, sir," he said. "Please accept this small gift for your inconvenience."

I turned the packet over in my hand. "This *is* a small gift," I said. "Do you happen to have one a little larger with, perhaps, a full set of camo gear, a face mask, a pair of hunting boots, and a double–barreled 12–gauge?" In eight hours, I was supposed to be sitting under a tree in full camouflage waiting for a Rio Grande gobbler. Even *with* a shotgun, I didn't think I'd much enjoy the experience dressed in light blue Dockers and sandals, which was what I was wearing. Without a shotgun, the whole thing seemed kind of silly.

After numerous phone calls (theirs) and some childish whining (mine), the baggage claims person promised to get my luggage on the next flight from Portland. Four hours later, I was finally groping for the thermostat in a cold motel room, and when John Lehnherr knocked on my door an hour after that and cheerfully called "Let's go huntin'," I hadn't even had time to work up a good case of morning breath.

Two cups of blistering–hot coffee, one for my lap and one for my stomach, and we were on our way through town. The weather, John explained, had been unseasonably warm and he suspected the wild turkeys had mated early. Normally, hunters do not talk about the breeding activities of birds any more than they talk about, say, a prostate biopsy which, incidentally, I had experienced just prior to this trip and which, as a matter of fact, may have been the *real* source of the bad luck. But if the toms had wrapped up their wooing activities for the year, they would be tough to bring to call—a process which uses a four–inch glass rod and a small, round slate to produce a variety of clucks, purrs, and yelps that are attractive to male turkeys. To me, the sounds are similar to those Lacey makes when she's squooshing around in the bathtub—wet skin on porcelain. It's supposed to make the old gobblers come running. They like that sort of stuff. I did, too—before the biopsy.

With the lights already off, John pulled his truck into a farm lane, reminded me to not slam the door, and in the blackness, we wordlessly felt our way along a rail fence. In a quarter mile, pasture gave way to the silhouettes of tall Douglas fir, and then I could smell the mountain laurel, the mint, and the ceanothus, and I knew we were on the fringe of a forest. We set down in a blackberry thicket directly beneath the largest fir and waited silently for the dawn.

When the sun was just squinting through the tanoak on the ridge above us, John made his first call. The only response was a loud, Velcro–like "r–r–r–i–ip–p–p" as I turned my head and a blackberry bramble caught my face mask and tore it from my head.

"Shhhh," John warned. In the truck, he had reminded me emphatically that silence and stealth were the essence of turkey hunting.

"Sorry," I called automatically and much too loudly. Next to me, my guide said nothing, but his shoulders hunched, and I heard a sucking sound much like the one I make when I crack my shin against the pew in church and want to cuss but can't. Then, I sneezed, and directly above us, a turkey gobbled violently, was challenged from another branch on the same tree, gobbled again, and was answered from yet another branch higher up. All in all, it was quite a thrilling event, and then three extremely large birds dropped like bombs from their perches and sailed off through the dim light. The hair on my arms didn't lay down again until my return flight, somewhere over the Cascades. We had set up under a roost tree!

John stood up and frowned. "Well that's a first," he said. "Just when you think you've got them all figured out. . . ." He made a feeble attempt to smile. "Bad luck all around," he said. "Let's go find another."

"Finding another," I quickly discovered, involved matching my well–used legs and abused lungs against those of a 29–year–old mountain man who had lived clean, probably never had a muscle spasm in his life, and wanted very much to find his client a turkey. It also meant following him to the top of the highest hill in southern Oregon. On the way, said client lassoed *two* charley horses and was deeply involved in some cotton–mouthed muttering, which included the philosophical "Do I really want a turkey *this* bad?"

At last, John stopped. A man of keen perception, he could tell through his binoculars that I was having difficulty keeping up. "Do you want to rest?" he called down the hill.

"Yaaarghhh," I replied feebly. "Neee waher."

"Water?"

"Yaaarghhh," I affirmed.

With his canteen open, John climbed down to where I leaned gasping against a stump. "Sorry about that," he said, extending the water. "I forget. We'll take it slow and quiet the rest of the way to the top. There's a real nice spot up there where I've seen a lot of sign."

"Do any of them say 'Cold Beer'?" I mumbled.

As miserable as I was then, less than a half hour later all distress was forgotten. Facing one–another, John and I were set up ten feet apart in knee–high ferns with our backs to manzanita trees. His slate call had brought an immediate response. Now, over his left shoulder and only three feet behind him I could see the red, white, and blue head of a huge Rio Grande gobbler. He was in an impossible spot for me to shoot, but oh, what a show as he fanned his tail, extended his wattled neck, and rattled off gobble after gobble! Then, as if that were not enough, *another* gobbler appeared over the same shoulder. The slightest movement, I knew, would cause them to disappear with a frightened "putt," so I remained silent and motionless for as long as I could, which was about 19 seconds. Then, the sweat in my eyes begged to be rubbed away, my elbow pleaded to be itched, and the crink in my lower back suggested I either extend a leg or suffer immediate and permanent paralysis. With all that talking going on, of course, the turkeys split, and to tell the truth, I was relieved. I was just about to enjoy a full–blown stretch when John, with a slight movement of one finger, indicated I should look to my left, which I did. Thirty–five yards away, a third gobbler was strutting through the ferns, oblivious to our presence. I raised my gun when he passed behind a yellow Scotch broom, and when the Fourth–of–July–colored head appeared on the other side, I fired.

John suggested later that I had missed, but I knew better. Hadn't I just told a friend from Florida it would be impossible to miss a turkey as he had done? Hadn't I scoffed at his excuses and questioned his eyesight, his virility, and his genetics? Hadn't I? Obviously, just as I pulled the trigger, an alien spacecraft had swooped down on that Oregon mountain top and swooped away again with my Thanksgiving dinner. There was not so much as a feather.

"Well," John said with a hint of dejection, "that about takes care of today. Tomorrow our luck will change." It did, too, but not the way he expected. John, you see, only knew about the bad luck at the airport. He didn't know I was riding out an epidemic.

The next two "tomorrows," in fact, have since become something of a stew with personal ineptitude, poor timing, paranoia and bad luck stirred in with the sweet smell of an Oregon forest in April, excellent fellowship, and several long–bearded toms. When I could sit still no longer, the turkeys came. When I was still, they came and I didn't see them. When I saw them, they saw me first. And when at last everything was perfect and a young tom strutted foolishly past me at 12 yards, my firing pin fell on an empty chamber. I'd forgotten to load my shotgun. Had been sitting around like that for hours.

On the last day, we awoke to a driving rain, and though John had located yet another bird and wanted me to try for it, I couldn't subject myself to further humiliation, for the bad luck was with me still. The evening before, we had separated to scout opposite sides of a mountain and I became disoriented. In a blind, panic–induced charge through head–high ceanothus, I had stumbled upon a sheep fence. Not until I was straddling it, did I determine it was electric, a revelation that caused me to cash in a whole bunch of fun tickets and forget a slew of other ailments besides. I had also spooked the gobblers I was supposed to be scouting, and later, lost my glasses forever somewhere in a 20x20–foot motel room.

"Let's call it a trip, John," I apologized, "my contribution to the economy of southern Oregon. I think this turkey hunting business means a heck of lot more to the turkeys than it does to me. Shoot, if I stayed any longer, I'd probably end up rolling around in one of those monstrous patches of poison oak I kept running into."

And so, I left my frustrated guide and flew back over the Cascades, returning the bad luck to its source in eastern Washington. My flight was uneventful, my luggage was at the airport when I arrived, and Lacey was but 40 minutes late picking me up. When the rash broke out the next morning, it only covered my upper torso—some good luck at last. The epidemic had run its course.

Close is good enough

A friend, Tom Allen, who is a pretty fair country shooter, can still not understand why wild game is served so infrequently at my house. "There's just no excuse for missing a shot like that," he is fond of telling me after I have muffed yet another broadside whitetail, or blown great holes in the air behind or in front of a Canada goose. But what does he know? Tom is a successful businessman who has spent a lifetime taking advantage of opportunities, catching planes, and showing up on time for graduations, weddings, and barbecues. I, on the other hand, have been practicing my missing since I blew a chance to take Arletta Dewlap to the fourth grade science fair. In one inglorious afternoon, I missed the first bus, then her stop, and finally the second step to her porch, winding up in a dentist's chair with a bruised ego and a chipped front tooth. My mother never forgave me for ruining my smile.

My junior high basketball coach was forever trying to impress upon his gangly, squeaky–voiced charges the importance of developing a winning tradition. "Basketball," he would tell us, "is an attitude. Get used to winning now and you'll be a winner all your life." Perhaps coincidentally, we were 0–20 that year.

The fact is, I have practiced missing for a long time. In high school, I missed a C– in Geometry by one point, just one of my numerous missed opportunities, points, and boats. My biology teacher, a sad, frustrated, purple–haired ogre named Miss Greymouth, suggested I had been standing behind the door when the brains were passed out, thus missing my chance to pass her class. This upset me some, for on the basketball court I generally missed all my free throws; it was not likely I would be drafted by the Celtics, but with a biology credit from Miss Greymouth's class I figured I could at least be a well–known gynecologist or brain surgeon.

Indeed, I have spent a lifetime preparing to be a poor shot. Even before my first slingshot, I had spent several years missing crows and alley cats with an assortment of hand–thrown dirt clods, pine cones, and crab apples. The truth is, though, I did not wish to hit those creatures; I threw because I thought I should, because little boys are expected by other little boys to do things like that. After a time, I became quite proficient at barely missing, a skill good enough to make me "one of the guys." No one suspected my errant throws were intentional. Later, when I became infatuated with heavy artillery and constructed a variety of propelling devices using everything from the elastic in my father's underwear to strips of bicycle tubing, it was even more imperative that I miss the "game" I stalked. A fellow could put a serious hurt on a prowling feline with a slingshot and a marble, and I didn't want that on my conscience. I'm still trying to figure out how I became a hunter, and I honestly think many of my "blown" shots today are actually subconscious concessions to my childhood philosophy that "close is good enough."

Why does an individual who will drive into the ditch to avoid hitting a family of grouse on the road even carry a gun in the first place? In the field during hunting season, those grouse are desirable targets and I will walk miles for a chance to miss them with a 20–gauge. Shooting game, I sometimes think, is largely a matter of challenge intensified by instinct, and though I have friends who've said it's a shame there's no such thing as shoot and release, I come darn close.

When I tried to explain all this to Tom last season, he

nodded sympathetically and suggested I should intentionally try to miss. The way he had it figured, that would put me right on target. Missing a miss, however, is a difficult concept to digest, and as yet, I have not been able to sort out the logistics. Most likely, I told him, it would cause me to miss by even more, and though a wide miss is difficult to distinguish from a narrow miss, I could not live with my instincts if I didn't think I was missing to the best of my ability.

Me, Woody, and that Pamela woman

It was not that I was so enraptured by my urban existence, but that I didn't know I had a choice. Conceived, born, nurtured, and schooled in the city, I just blindly accepted the fact that some lived on one side of the town boundary, some lived on the other, and I, by tradition, was a city boy. And while I envied the lifestyle of my few rural friends, it occurred to me rather late in life that I, as well as the next guy, could build a home away from sirens, garbage pickup, door–to–door solicitors, and cable television.

Even with that realization, ours began as a vacation place, a modest "escape." In the beginning, we were talking log cabin—not log house—a weekend project that would take a couple years and but a few thousand dollars. But we drew up a plan and the plan got bigger. We cut and peeled logs and decided we needed more. And before we could say "Lincoln log syndrome," Lacey and I were so far beyond the point of no return it was easier to see where we were going than where we had come from. We sold our house next to the shopping mall, built a beautiful, two–story, log home near Loon Lake, and moved in ten months after we started. So much for a vacation place. So much for a couple thousand dollars.

Our resolve to adapt to non–urban living was immediately challenged. Awakening at dawn less than a week after the move, I had the foggy notion Mr. Ginrich was banging on the wall. "Okay, okay," I called out sleepily, "I'll turn the volume down!"

"Alan," Lacey reminded me as her elbow found the soft part under my ribs, "we haven't had a landlord since we were first married."

"Then why is he still banging on our walls?" I mumbled, rubbing some of the sleep away.

"Alan," Lacey said more patiently, "I think there's a woodpecker on the house."

Tentatively, I crept from our mattress and peered into the gloom. Nothing. The noise had ceased, but while I weighed the advantages of an early breakfast versus another hour of sleep, it began again and I identified the culprit as he flicked from one log to another: Lacey was right—a woodpecker. So! We really *had* forsaken the city. Somehow this bird made it official, and I was pleased.

At five the next morning, the rapping began again, right above my head, but this time I lay there enjoying the beat. It had been a lousy dream anyway, and being awakened by a woodpecker was a lot more aesthetic than being awakened by sirens or clanging garbage cans. Smiling, I pictured the pileated fowl out there on the house rattling his little brains against the logs. Ten minutes later, though, the persistent rat–a–tat–tat had not subsided and was becoming more difficult to appreciate. I slapped my hand against the pine paneling and the noise stopped. Certain he had fled, I turned over and pulled the covers around my ears.

In ten minutes, Woody was back, snapping me awake, and this time I was upset. Pamela Sue Anderson had just begged me to show her my collection of Federal duck stamps. Again, I slapped my hand against the wall. The hammering ceased momentarily, then resumed again. Two more forceful whacks broke a blood vessel in my palm. Rising reluctantly to soak my bruise in cold water, my inclinations were leaning more toward revenge than passive coexistence; normally, Pamela Sue would not give me the time of day. Then, just when things were getting interesting, that bird wakes me up.

I ate breakfast and went outside to see what the pesky creature had found so fascinating. There was a hole in my new logs! That woodpecker was eating my house!

During the next week, I took passive, humanitarian measures to prevent a violent showdown, but the bird interpreted my docility for resignation or weakness. Until that time, I had no inherent animosity toward woodpeckers; indeed, Woody had been one of my favorite childhood cartoon characters, but each morning this relative of his was there outside the bedroom window thumbing his beak at me while drilling unsightly holes

in the logs that represented ten months of blisters and sweat. Still, I wanted to be civilized about the whole thing. Figuring he was merely looking for a home, I constructed a bird house where his drilling was concentrated. Disregarding the opening already provided, however, he pecked one through the side and started again on my logs.

Next, I talked to an ornithologist about Woody's activities and was told he was probably just looking for insect larva in the logs.

There are no insect larva in my logs, I explained. They have been treated to prevent that very thing. Perhaps he doesn't know that, I was told. Perhaps after a few more exploratory holes he will figure it out. I don't want more exploratory holes, I said. Those logs represent a big chunk of my life and I am developing bags under my eyes from loss of sleep. What are my chances with Pamela Sue Anderson if I have bags under my eyes? Probably just as good as without bags, he told me, proving once again that fancy titles have nothing to do with diplomacy.

Becoming more desperate as the woodpecker grew bolder, I schemed to drive him away, arranging an arsenal of loud, but non–lethal, Fourth of July leftovers on my nightstand. The next time the rapping began, I groggily lit one and heaved it out the window. Unfortunately, my observation that the window was open was incorrect, resulting in a charred carpet and the loss of one eyebrow. Then, in desperation after a particularly short night, I slipped from my bed and stumbled into the yard clad only in my briefs. Scooping up a handful of driveway gravel, I tried to sluice my scansorial pest from the side of the house. The pebbles spread out in a real nice pattern, shattering the bedroom window. This sent Lacey clamoring for the phone to report a break–in. Then she noticed I was gone, and she reported a kidnapping, too. Unaware of all this, I appropriated my nephew's BB gun from the woodshed where his parents had hidden it, and when the two officers arrived, I was crouched like an assassin behind a honeysuckle bush hoping for a shot at the bird.

Quite naturally, the officers were nervous to find a 200–pound man in much–too–tight mauve and teal Fruit of the Loom briefs crouching in the bushes with a gun in his hands, and I was equally nervous that my congenial, "How ya doin'?" didn't put them at ease. When we finally got everything sorted out, however, Lacey was giggling, the police were having coffee in the kitchen, the woodpecker was still tapping merrily away, and I was on my way to town for some log–colored silicone and a pair of ear plugs. Critters, I decided, were part of the country package, and a deficient truce was better than an ineffectual war. Maybe with the plugs, I could at least get enough sleep to entice that Pamela woman to come back and look at my duck stamps.

Janie McGee is a good kid

Last week, in a paroxysm of nostalgia, I cut a forked willow stick, sliced some strips from an old bicycle tube, removed the tongue from a pair of boat shoes, and made myself a slingshot. Afterwards, Lacey mentioned that if my time was worth anything, I could have bought a slingshot for $50 and been money ahead, but saving money wasn't my motivation; I've waited a long time to be old enough to do silly, impractical things just because I want to, and I must say the slingshot has provided me immeasurably more pleasure than the shelves I built in the fruit room.

This week, my cousin's youngest daughter, Janie, and I have been taking the slingshot for walks down by the slough that runs into the woods north of my house, and so far we've cold–cocked a couple African lions, turned a hard–charging white rhino, and let the pterodactyls in the neighborhood know who's boss. When the season comes along and I've figured out all the ballistics and such, we're going after something more challenging—like the blue grouse on the big hill above the sawmill. It's been a long time since I pulled a slingshot and Janie never has before, and we can't decide whether to sight through the bottom or top of the "V," or whether to even sight at all. Trusting to luck is okay for a charging white rhino, but we wouldn't want to blow a chance at a big blue grouse. So far, we know a perfectly round stone will shoot ten times straighter than an irregular one, and that if you value your knuckles you'll make sure the bands aren't twisted and the ammunition is centered in the pouch.

Today, Janie and I went out again to patrol the perimeter with our slingshot. Janie, who is eight, is a good kid and very perceptive for her age. That's why I like her so much. She told her mother I was the smartest man in the world because I know where clouds go and mosquitoes come from. (The answer is northern British Columbia). When Janie is with me, all kinds of exciting things happen because she catches on fast and is great at letting me spot game.

"Look at that grouse, Janie," I said to her. "There, on the second limb of that biggest aspen."

Janie looked. "That's an old wasp nest, silly," she said.

"No, no, Janie," I insisted. "It's a brown–phase ruff grouse. Look at him spread his tail feathers."

Janie looked again and remembered the game. "Oh, I see him now," she said, "but look on the limb above that one, Uncle Alan. There's a big 'ol gobbler sittin' there."

"That's not a gobbler," I said. "That's a Himalayan snow cock."

Janie giggled and shook her head. Then she put her hands on her hips and looked exasperated. "The snow cock is four branches up. The gobbler is between it and the grouse." She whispered out of the side of her mouth. "Do ya think you can get him, Uncle Alan?" and that settled any question of identification; it was definitely a gobbler.

Slowly, I drew back the rubber. My roundest rock, chosen the day before expressly for wild gobblers by Janie L. McGee was nestled in the pouch.

"Hurry, Uncle Alan, he's going to fly!"

"Twaaang!"

"You missed!"

"I did?"

"Shoot again," she insisted. "He's still there!"

I fumbled in my pocket for another stone. "Twaaang."

"You missed again!"

"I did not."

"He's flying, Uncle Alan! Get him or we won't have any supper!"

Again, I reloaded quickly. "Twaaang! Whuppp!" A small, leafy twig, severed from high above, dropped through the branches and hit the ground.

Janie ran to it and held it aloft with both hands. "Supper!" she called exuberantly, and I grinned and bowed, and prepared to make a speech. "That was a tough shot, huh, Uncle Alan?" she said.

"The toughest," I said modestly.

"But you wanted to give him a chance, huh, Uncle Alan?" she said.

I wasn't sure if it was a declaration or a question, so I nodded just in case. We completed the loop through the woodlot, but I kept the slingshot in my back pocket. It felt good there—as it had 40 years before when I was Janie's age.

Tonight at the dinner table, Janie will tell her folks about my great shot, and her dad will hear the story and smile. The next time he runs into me at the post office, he'll joke about my "gobbler." Hopefully, Ralph, the post master, will be close enough to pick up a few key words. Then, Ralph will tell Arty Davis, who thinks he is the only fellow in these parts who knows sic–em about hunting turkeys. Won't he be surprised to learn otherwise! As I said, Janie McGee is a good kid.

Finding rhinos

I first began to suspect I was losing my hearing five years ago. A spring squall roared across Priest Lake as Wes Graham and I were returning from an early morning fishing trip. Caught at mid–lake in a 12–foot boat, rain slashing our backs, we decided our best chance was to outrun the inevitable white-caps. Two hundred yards from safety, however, just when I figured we had it made, Wes began hollering, and from where I cowered in the bow, I distinctly heard him yell, "Abandon ship!" So I did.

"Now that was different," Wes said when he had circled back to drag my sodden body over the gunwhale. "Why'd you do that?"

"You said to abandon ship," I shivered. "I figured you knew something I didn't."

Shaking his head in disbelief, Wes eased the small craft into shallow water and the shelter of a cove. "What I said was 'Let 'er rip!'" he told me. "The wind was really kicking up behind us, but I knew we were going to make it." He looked at me as a mother looks at a son who has destroyed her kitchen trying to surprise her with breakfast. "You really ought to have your ears checked, buddy."

"Whaddaya mean, have my ears checked!" I answered defensively as I shucked my soggy life vest. "One little mis-communication and I'm ready for a hearing aid? Is that what you think? In case you don't remember, fella, it was darn chaotic out there. Anyone could have made that mistake."

Wes smiled thinly, shook his head, and dug under the back seat, mumbling something about finding rhinos.

"Rhinos?" I said. "Rhinos? Are you out of your mind? We're in North America, fer cryin' out loud!"

"Dry clothes!" Wes said, enunciating carefully. "I said we should find you some dry clothes."

"You did not," I said sheepishly. "I heard you perfectly."

Wes dug around some more and tossed me a sweatshirt. "Well, then," he said sarcastically, "shall we?"

"Shall we what?"

"Find some rhinos?"

It is indeed ironic—one of those little life jokes like baldness and gum disease—that hunting, the very thing that makes my life complete, has also given me the auditory discrimination of a railroad tie. I was 16 when I first picked up a sporting arm, and in the 35 years since, I conservatively estimate I have pulled the trigger 15,000 times. That's a lot of noise. The 500 firecrackers I touched off in my Aunt Ruthie's metal machine shed when I was ten didn't help either, my audiologist tells me, but I really should have been using some sort of hearing protection all along, and for not doing so, I plead stupid.

"It's like this," Dr. Huston said as he cast a critical eye over my audiogram. "You have a rather severe loss in both ears. Sensorineural. Nerve deafness. It's the most common. Do you work around heavy equipment?"

"Only Betta Bunwad," I said. "She'll go maybe 280." I thought for a moment. "Of course, there's Mrs. Sweat in bookkeeping, but she's been on a diet and. . . ."

"What about the Service?" the doctor interrupted as he put a check on my chart. "Were you in the Service?"

"Four years," I replied.

Doctor Huston smiled knowingly and checked his chart again. "Army?" he asked.

"Forest," I replied.

"What?"

"The Forest Service. Up by Sullivan Lake."

Dr. Huston erased the check and put one in a different

column. “And I suppose while in the Forest Service you worked with a chainsaw?” he said, smiling hopefully.

“Nope,” I replied. “I pulled ribes.”

“What?” The doctor slipped a finger under his glasses and rubbed one eye vigorously.

“Ribes. Wild gooseberries,” I explained. “The host plant for white pine blister rust.” I looked at him skeptically. “Say, Doc, that’s the second time I’ve repeated myself. When’s the last time you had *your* hearing checked?”

Dr. Huston seemed to momentarily lose his composure. “And what difference does a wild gooseberry make?” he asked irritably.

“Like I started to explain, Doc,” I said, “if there isn’t a host, there isn’t blister rust, and if there isn’t blister rust, there isn’t a canker, and without a canker, the tree won’t be girdled and die. It’s all pretty simple—sort of a no–host affair, if you will. Say,” I asked, “what’s all this got to do with nerve deafness? Are you by any chance charging by the hour?”

“By the hour?”

“That’s what I said, Doc, and I don’t think *you* are hearing so well yourself today. “That’s *three* times now.”

Dr. Huston got up, removed his glasses, and wiped them absently on his white frock. “As a matter of fact, I *do* wear a hearing aid,” he said. “Perhaps I need to make some adjustments, because I’m really not making much sense of what you. . . .” His voice drifted off. “Can you come back tomorrow?” he asked.

“Can’t do ‘er tomorrow,” I said. “I’m going duck hunting. How about Monday?”

“Monday is my day off, but. . . did you say duck hunting?” He brightened just a little. “With a shotgun?”

“No, Doc,” I joked, “I just sneak up on ‘em with a roll of duct tape and. . . .” I was about to continue the jest, but the good doctor’s lower lip fell so far I feared he would trip on it, and I decided not to torment him further.

In the end, it was Dr. Huston who almost had the last laugh: he said for $1160 he could solve all my auditory problems, and he fitted me for two in–the–ear hearing aids and a set of cus-

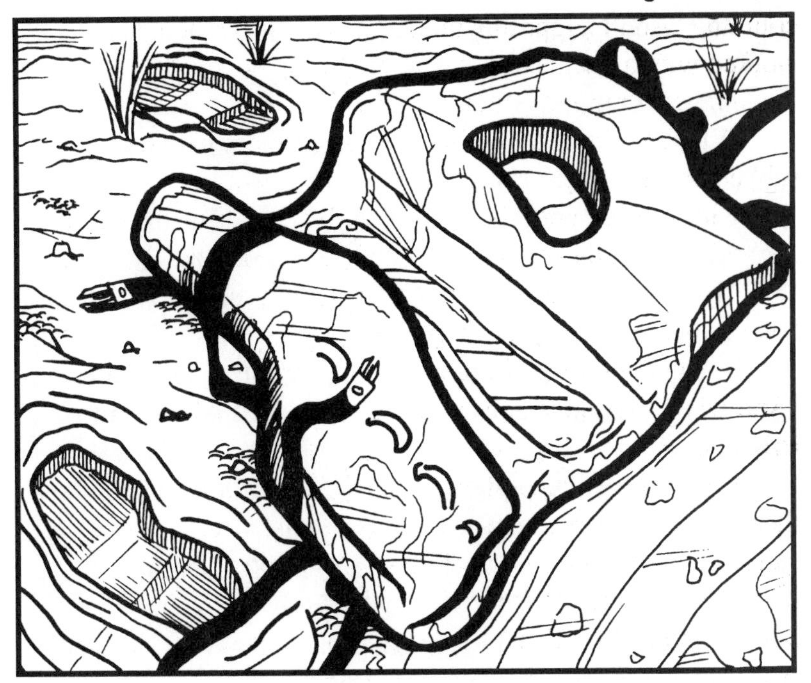

tom–molded noise reducers. For $550 each, I would get devices to amplify sound, and for another $60, I would get noise–reducing plugs to keep the sound out.

The hearing aids, he said, were to be worn faithfully, as they would take some getting use to. Sounds which had for years been beyond my audio discriminatory capacity—like running refrigerators, bad rear bearings, and Lacey's grumbling about the condition of the yard—would come in again, loud and clear. The plugs, on the other hand, would prevent further damage to my already–abused inner ear when I was exposed to loud noises like shotgun blasts, boat motors, and Lacey's angry shrieking when I came home late for important dinner engagements wearing muddy hip boots and a grin. It was important, the doctor warned me with a chuckle, to not confuse the aids with the plugs as they were similar in appearance.

"You won't want to be wearing the hearing aids when you fire your shotgun," he smiled, "as you can imagine how *that* would sound." Having gained control once again, Doc Huston was in a much better frame of mind.

"But with the plugs in, will I be able to hear a pair of pintails whistling in from behind the blind?" I asked.

"What?"

"Pintails," I repeated. "Sprigs. Ducks. You know—quack, quack."

"Quack quack?" Doctor Huston eyed me critically, then shot a glance toward the door. "Quack quack?" he said again.

"That's what I said, Doc," I nodded. "Though with a pintail it's more of a whistle. Will I be able to hear it?"

"Probably not," he said, still looking confused. "The reducers will let in many sounds, but you'll lose some of the more subtle ones."

"Then maybe I'd better wear aids in the blind," I decided.

"But not when you shoot," he clucked.

"Have you ever been duck hunting, Doc?" I asked.

"No."

"I didn't think so." I looked at him seriously and couldn't help myself. "How 'bout Doc hunting, duck?"

"What?"

"There you go again with that 'What?' business," I said, shaking my head. "How 'bout if I just keep 'em turned off."

"What?"

"HOW ABOUT I JUST KEEP 'EM TURNED OFF?" I said again, louder.

Doctor Huston shook his head, pushed his hand through his thick hair, and nervously eyed the door again. "If you do that, you will have negated the purpose of hearing aids entirely. It wouldn't be wise, would it, to pay $1,100 for a pair of ear plugs? In fact, it would be really dumb."

"Well, with the aids, will I be able to hear the music when Wes puts in his old Beach Boys tapes on the drive to the duck pond? I asked.

"Definitely."

"What about his humming?"

"That, too," the doctor beamed. "You'll hear things you've been missing for years."

"I was afraid of that," I said.

"What?"

"I was afraid of that!" I repeated loudly.

The doctor covered his ears and grimaced. "A little less volume, please," he pleaded. "I can hear you just fine."

"Well, you sure don't act like it," I said, shuffling through the literature on his desk. "Just a couple more questions, Doc," I said finally. "Can I get the hearing aids wet?"

"Definitely not," he said.

"And I should wear the plugs rather than the aids when I'm around an outboard engine?"

"That is correct."

"So what you're saying is, I won't be able to hear Wes next time he says 'Let 'er rip!' even if I do own hearing aids?"

"What?"

"And if I do wear them and I hear him, I'll also be amplifying the sound of the outboard, which isn't good for my ears, but on the other hand, I'll probably not think he said 'Find some rhinos' when he said 'Find some dry clothes'."

Doctor Huston was edging toward his door. "I've got to be going," he mumbled as he reached for the knob.

"Okay by me, Doc," I called. "Stop in again, though, and we'll see if we can't adjust that hearing aid of yours." When he was gone, I tore up my check. Then, I put my feet up on the good doctor's desk. He wasn't exactly a walking testimonial for his product, this Doc Huston, and I suspected his powder was a mite wet besides. I figured I could get on a few more years with just the noise reducers, and for that, a couple pieces of wadded toilet paper would just have to do.

The metal conspiracy

My faithful pickup quit running last month on the way home from a weekend crappie fishing expedition. An '88, extended cab 4x4 with over 190,000 miles, he had performed flawlessly since his purchase, surviving an unfortunate collision with a very large mule deer and also a stretch of black Interstate ice that put him on his back like a turtle and caused my insurance company to write me a series of nasty letters. Then, 45 miles from the nearest phone on a night so nasty the moon had called in sick, he just quit. No whimper, no wheeze, no hiccup. Just the ominous sound of crunching gravel as he rolled to a stop.

Possessing the God–given mechanical aptitude of a turnip, I got out of my truck and did my usual turnipy things—lifting the hood, kicking the tires, checking for rocks under the hub caps and rust under the fenders. Then, I got back in, crossed my fingers, started him up, and drove home without a sputter. Three minutes, no reason, and we have since gone 2500 miles without a problem. What's the story?

I am convinced there is a conspiracy among metal objects with moving parts to keep me humble by occasionally reminding me I am at the mercy of their whims. I think there is a network of trucks and lawn mowers and rototillers and barbecue rotisseries dedicated to preventing me from becoming happily complacent. Each time I experience the first tinglings of confidence in the use of one or another, one or another will stop functioning, and always at the most inopportune times. While I am uncertain of their motivation, I suspect it is somehow tied in with the fact that at one time in my careless past, I was a chronic abuser of anything with moving parts made of metal, and they are now exacting revenge.

Being far more interested in why dogs pointed and how trout held so easily in a strong current, it was many years before I even took the time to learn the basics of fishing equipment maintenance, and I loved a fly reel, I really did. Cars, too, I treated as a mere assemblage of nuts and bolts for taking me fishing, and I drove two to death before I ever learned the importance of changing oil. Granted, they were not expensive reels or expensive cars, and in an ugly fight they'd have been used for ammunition, but had I offered them minimal care, they would have at least looked better when they died; I feel bad about that. Lawn mowers, snow blowers, and other mechanical devices that reeked of toil, of course, I abused even worse, but even now I have a hard time working up any guilt when I forget to put them in the garage after use.

Nowadays, I clean and oil my fishing reels regularly, keep them in cloth cases when not in use, and hardly ever drag them through gravel or sand. Despite this TLC, however, there have been times when they have turned on me. The worst I can remember was on a fly–in fishing trip on the Alaska Peninsula where, because of my own stupidity and a mix–up at the outfitters, I found myself on the best trout lake in creation with only one rod and reel. Fortunately, I caught a bragging–size fish on my first cast, because after that the reel froze up and stopped doing what reels are designed to do.

Okay, I told myself, here is a chance to spend a week photographing fish and wildlife without the worry of missing out on any personal action. With that noble concession, I quickly happened upon a sow grizzly batting spawned–out sockeye from a small feeder creek to a cub which waited greedily on the rock–strewn bank. Great stuff, and with my wide–angle lens, I could get it all. To make things even better, a look through the viewfinder showed a band of caribou feeding within the same frame. In all the years I had been wandering about with a 35 millimeter camera, that was absolutely the best photo opportunity I had ever experienced, and had the camera shutter not stuck, I'm sure those pictures would have made me rich and famous.

As it was, I probably guaranteed myself continued bedevilment by things mechanical, but nothing as ill–humored as that camera deserved to go on a nice fishing trip ever again. I took great care to leave the Alaska tundra exactly as I had found it, but if you ever fly through Clark Pass, hang a left at Iliamna, and set down on a little lake that looks like an hour glass, you might see my 35 millimeter near the west shoreline. It's in eight feet of crystal–clear water.

Dear Mrs. Halvorson:

You might not remember me, but maybe you remember my brother–in–law, Thayer the Abnormal. We had breakfast in your little cafe about five months ago on the way to some walleye fishing on the river, and Thayer spilled the pancake syrup on your big yellow tabby, Beastie. I was the tall guy with the fly swatter who tried to dislodge her from Thayer's head.

I want to tell you again, Mrs. Halvorson, that I really have nothing against cats. As a child, I had several, mostly because my folks wouldn't let me have a dog, but I would have never taken a swat at Beastie had not Thayer insisted she was eating his ear. To tell you the truth, Ma'am, I admire cats a heck of a lot more than I admire my brother–in–law, but my sister kind of likes him and thinks his ears are cute, which is fortunate, because the rest of him is elbow ugly.

Anyway, after we got the blood stopped and the cat finished running around in my pancakes, you brought us big slices of apple pie with some kind of a caramel topping. Now, I haven't had pie for breakfast since my bachelor days, and what I did have then was of the frozen, cardboardy variety where you can't find the fruit for anything and you're not sure what you've got until you read the label on the box. Ma'am—yours was the best apple pie I have ever eaten, and I hope I told you so at the time. Now, Christmas Eve is at my house this year and there's about a jillion relatives coming over. The kids will probably be too involved in the package–opening frenzy to eat dessert, but I do think the rest of us could do some serious damage to a half–dozen Mrs. Halvorson apple pies.

We always have wild roast goose for Christmas Eve dinner, and usually it turns out pretty good. I'm trying something a little different this year with a dutch oven and some Cabernet Sauvignon, however, and I was also wondering what spice it was you used to give your Chicken Supreme such a distinctive flavor. Is it basil? I'd like to try it with my goose. I had chicken in your place last year right after that big wind storm in December. I was soaking wet and you let me and three other duck hunters sit in the kitchen by the bread oven and eat dinner in our long underwear. There was a little commotion when one of the fellows got so comfortable he forgot he was half naked and padded off with a smile to the lavatory through the Saturday night dinner crowd, but you sent the constable home with a laugh and a big hunk of hot raisin bread dripping with real butter.

Raisin bread, by the way, is one of my favorites, and I must say yours makes me envious. My wife, Lacey, bought me a bread machine for my birthday, and I'm having a lot of fun with it, but I have had no success whatsoever with some of the recipes. I made a loaf of raisin bread a couple weeks ago and it was so heavy we had to throw it to the dogs. Dude, the Lab, got the lion's share, and later, when I took him for a swim, he could barely keep his nose above water. Believe me, Mrs. Halvorson, there is nothing quite so pathetic as the look on the face of a "water dog" that suddenly realizes he is going under. Do you put the raisins in your bread before, after, or during kneading? And what about the water? Do you think it should be hot, or is warm good enough? Lacey says my yeast isn't doing what it's supposed to be doing, but I don't know if that's my fault or the yeast's. I have a lot of things that don't do what they're supposed to.

I noticed last December that you didn't have fruit cake on your menu. I don't particularly care for fruit cake, but during the holidays, I'll bet you could sell a lot of it. Most people eat the stuff because you're *supposed* to during the holidays, just like you're supposed to eat hard boiled eggs at Easter and black jelly beans at Halloween. My Uncle Pat had a recipe for a rum cake passed down from *his* Uncle Pat and *his* Uncle Pat before him. I could get you the recipe if you like, but I can't guarantee how good it is because there was a water mark on the paper and none of the Pats ever got past the first line. They all thought the recipe said to *chug* a bottle of dark Jamaican rum, whereas it actually said to *chill* a bottle.

If this letter appears to be rambling, Mrs. Halvorson, the reason is that I've been getting up my nerve. Yes, we truly would like to have your pies for dessert Christmas Eve, yes, I would like to try a new recipe with my goose, and yes, my raisin bread was a dismal failure. I even had an Uncle Pat. I see in the paper, Ma'am, that you had a Pat, too, and that he passed away just a month ago after a prolonged illness. I'm very sorry. I have spent a few Christmas Eve's alone when I didn't want to, Mrs. Halvorson, and I wouldn't wish that on anyone. We're not kin, you and I, but I feel we should be. You and your little cafe have provided some of my most comfortable memories over the years. Lacey and I and our jillions of relatives would be honored if you would join us for Christmas Eve. And about those pies—Lacey says to come early, and we'll do them together in the kitchen.

Our Sincerest Holiday Wishes,

Alan Liere

Camper fever

I suppose I should be thankful I got in as much fishing as I did and that I'm not locked up in some Canadian jail. When my brother–in–law, Thayer, first crashed through the back door of that little cafe at Dease Lake, British Columbia, with gobs of cantaloupe splattered against his left temple and dripping from an eyebrow, he was screaming for the Mounties, the constable, and the Humane Society. As yet, he's not talking to me, which I don't mind a bit, but my wife (his sister) isn't either, and I miss Lacey when she's not in a decent mood.

Thayer still insists the incident was premeditated and malicious, and that anyone who would try to terminate a relative with a ripe cantaloupe deserves to be behind bars. His accusations, of course, are ridiculous. The truth is, I have never in my life been so fortunate to purchase a ripe cantaloupe; it was over–ripe. Rather than whining, he should be counting his blessings, for had my selection been hard and green as it usually is, it would have done some major damage. My intent was only to call his attention to the fact we had become incompatible and to encourage him to catch a plane home. Had I been able to make this point by throwing something else—say a small cluster of seedless grapes or a pint of German potato salad—I might have done so.

It was supposed to have been *my* vacation. For three years, I had been promising myself a fishing orgy in the Yukon—an elaborate and extended pat on the back for surviving my belated return to college and the accompanying fatigue, headaches, and recurring tendency to question whether anyone over 40 can actually be considered a living organism on five hours sleep per night. Darn it, I needed that vacation and I wanted to go alone! Furthermore, my camper was one of those small, molded fiberglass jobs fitted to the chassis of a four–cylinder truck. With barely enough space to sneeze, it made no sense at all to take Thayer with me. If he hadn't brazenly appealed to my inherent distrust of moving metal, I wouldn't have, either.

Thayer Bogg is like a mosquito; though his existence is undeniable, the logic behind his creation is suspect. Were it not for his uncanny mechanical ability, in fact, he would have been slapped into oblivion long ago. Among his numerous irritations is the fact he is an expert in practically everything. Just ask him. Learning to tie a Wooly Worm or Doc Spratly? Thayer can help. Rewinding the ferrules on a fly rod? He can do it better. Pondering whether to invest in metals or commodities? Thayer can advise you. It matters not that his Wooly Worm looks like the love child of an illicit affair between a magpie and a summer coyote. It matters not that most men—even one–handed—could wind and secure a garden hose around a croquet mallet more artistically than he rewinds a ferrule, or that the only investment he has ever made in metal futures is the garbage sack of empty, aluminum beer cans in his garage.

Like most, I have a tendency to admire in others those areas in which I am personally deficient, and of all my deficiencies, mechanical ineptness is most conspicuous. I feel I have accomplished something magical when I turn a key and my truck coughs reluctantly to life. I am thrilled each time my lawn mower starts and absolutely ecstatic when I successfully attach two boards together with a bolt, a washer, and one of those little hexagon thingies you twist using one of those adjusting devices that changes its gap in the middle of the job and makes you curse. As a youth, I simultaneously destroyed the engine *and* transmission of my first car attempting to change the oil. I buy cheap, plastic fishing reels because the innards of *any* fishing reel terrifies me, and I would rather throw one away than open it up to make repairs. I'm still looking for a disposable vehicle.

"So yer goin' to the Yukon, huh?" Thayer stood in the driveway, arms folded across his chest, rocking on his heels.

"Uh huh," I muttered laconically, wishing he would wander off and torment someone else.

"How long you figure to be gone?" he asked, sliding closer to where I was stashing boxes of food and fishing gear in the already– overloaded camper.

"About five weeks," I muttered.

"There's some pretty nasty roads up there," he grinned happily. "Ya think this rig will make it?"

"Should," I said.

"Well what if it don't? Service stations are few and far between." He was almost drooling with delight. "And they say a man what breaks down up there can figure on stayin' a piece."

I tried to look unconcerned, but Thayer had shot a verbal arrow into my Achilles heel and I could tell he knew it. "What's that supposed to mean?" I asked, knowing good and

well what it was supposed to mean. Thayer was inviting himself along on *my* vacation. Furthermore, after planting the seed, he knew my inherent fear of mechanical failure virtually guaranteed him a spot in the passenger's seat.

Two days later, we were on our way, the camper belly almost dragging the pavement in its fullness, Thayer already getting on my nerves as he instructed me on a shortcut out of town that added ten minutes to the drive. After only a few miles, however, he was blessedly asleep, and I was grinning wryly at my wife's assurance that "At least you'll have someone to talk to." Thayer snored soundly, though one unaccustomed to such an assortment of snorts, gurgles, and wheezes would have sworn a St. Bernard with asthma was playing with a soda straw in a bucket of milk.

Many miles later, at the Canadian border, Thayer came awake long enough to whistle the "Star Spangled Banner" as the customs agent asked the usual questions about destination and length of stay. I'm not sure the whistling had anything to do with the fact my vehicle was then subjected to a thorough search during which I had to forfeit a bag of groceries and a good bottle of bourbon, but it probably didn't help, and the systematic ransacking would possibly have gone faster if Thayer hadn't in the process bombarded the agent with questions about smugglers, counterfeiters, and illegal aliens.

Not too long after crossing the border, we stopped to sample the fishing, but Thayer had stepped on my spinning rod while storing his own and had "forgotten" to mention it. Though I caught several respectable trout, I didn't find it very enjoyable without a rod tip. Thayer, of course, explained "any fool can repair somethin' like that," but after his emergency repairs on my outfit, I decided to buy a new one at the next town; two pounds of electrician's tape on a rod tip really messes up the action.

Miles and miles later, we turned onto the Cassiar Highway, and Thayer and I began stopping to fish at nearly every stream, river, slough, lake, and beaver pond. Some of these had fish and some didn't, but we were experiencing beautiful weather and spectacular scenery, and I was more than content to let intentions of "a couple quick casts" drift into hours during which I savored the solitude of the days and tried to unwind from nightmare nights in a small camper, pinned to the window by a snoring brother–in–law whose gnashing teeth and violent nocturnal thrashings made sleep impossible.

Eventually, we came to the beautiful Iskut Valley, fishing lakes with names like Eddontenajon, Tatogga, and Kinasken. The weather became dark and drizzly, but nothing could dampen my enthusiasm for this adventure. Thayer, though, was another story. Whereas before, he had tested my endurance mainly at night, he now set out to ruin my days as well. Mosquitoes, damp clothing, unlevel camping spots, and my cooking were sources of his lament, but not until the afternoon he complained of boredom and switched on the truck radio did I react to his irrational behavior. Calmly, I switched it off. Smiling fiendishly, he switched it back on, glared at me hatefully, and began an off–key rendition of "North to Alaska" that would have gagged even the grizzled gold rushers of the Klondike. As pleasantly as possible, I suggested he not besmear the good name of Johnny Horton, and then tried to stuff the contents of a litter bag in his mouth. He retaliated by sucking his teeth.

As the rains continued, Thayer and I became even less compatible in that small camper. He spent hours just staring at me, then making faces behind my back. Though I never caught him at it, I could tell by his innocent smile what he was doing. Because of the moisture, it was necessary to change clothes frequently, and after a few more days, the camper was strewn with molding socks, steaming wool shirts, and dripping corduroys. I was convinced Thayer was sneaking dry underwear from my duffel, and he had already monopolized the best hanging spots for his own wet clothes. When he intentionally hung his dripping jacket where it would saturate my pillow, I got back by planting a 14–inch trout in his sleeping bag. The next morning, my toothbrush and prescription laxative were not to be found. Thayer made much an ado about helping me look for them, but I knew he had hidden them during the night. This became even more obvious after breakfast as I enviously watched him head, smirking, toward a roadside outhouse with a roll of toilet paper. That, I suppose, was the beginning of the end, but I'm certain things would not have gotten so hostile if Thayer had been able to repair the fuel pump.

"How long will it take to fix?" I asked, jamming my head alongside his under the hood and staring without comprehension into the tangled confusion of metal and wires and little things that go up and down and in and out.

Thayer stepped back and wiped his hands on the tail of my shirt. "'Bout an hour," he said confidently. "Any simpleton can put in a fuel pump." He paused and looked at me crookedly. "That's assumin', of course, you got an extra fuel pump."

"What do they look like?" I asked, hopefully holding up a spare oil filter.

"Don't worry about it, brother–in–law," he said. "You ain't got it. I'd best hitchhike into Dease Lake and pick one up." He extended his hand. "Gimme yer credit card."

Thayer caught a ride back to Dease Lake almost immediately, and after seeing him off, I splashed back to the camper in a drenching rain. It was locked. Thayer had the key. I was upset. Five hours later, I was also very wet.

Thayer never did show up. Eventually, I hitch–hiked to Dease Lake myself, though *I* was not picked up immediately. When I found him, he was sitting in the A&M Restaurant guzzling hot coffee, munching a warm cinnamon roll, and entertaining the clientele with *his* lies and *my* credit card. That's when I went next door and bought the cantaloupe. Like I said, he was fortunate it was not hard and green. I don't guess there's any sense in telling my wife it was the only one they had.

JuJu Perdicious and the Christmas tree massacre

For the rest of us, it was no big deal. The money was nice, but we probably would have gotten along okay without it. I mean, it wasn't like we had any girl friends to support or anything. But Juju Perdicious—that was a different story. JuJu accepted employment to circumvent an atrocity—namely his murder at the hands of his old man.

Pop Deleganes was old (about 45) but he wasn't JuJu's old man. Pop owned the biggest Christmas tree plantation in Stevens County, Washington—Douglas fir—some of the finest in the state. "The rest of us" were Eddie Shawgo, Dennis Valentine, Jeff Hanks, and myself—all on the hairless side of 15. Pop had hired us as tree pruners, armed us with machetes, and charged us with trimming and shaping the reckless spring growth into symmetrical, saleable, trees. It was pleasant work until JuJu came along. Then things got ugly.

We all knew JuJu, but we hadn't paid him much mind. He was older and had never been part of our group because he didn't hunt or fish, and he wore his hair too long. Also, he had a girl friend, Bonnie Lee Bedsach, while the rest of us merely talked about such soft, sacred wonders in envious whispers.

We didn't dislike JuJu, but we hadn't been able to relate to him, and secretly we wondered what kind of parents would name their kid "JuJu."

Another terrible thing about JuJu was that he didn't yet have a driver's license. Every other red–blooded American boy of our acquaintance got a driver's license the day he turned 16, but JuJu Perdicious had failed his test nine times in a year and a half. This was fortunate, as JuJu couldn't drive, and *that* was the reason he came to work at the Christmas tree plantation. JuJu, you see, had "borrowed" his father's Oldsmobile to take Bonnie Lee for a spin. When he rolled it, he simply walked home and went to bed. He tried to act surprised the next morning when his father discovered the car was not in the garage, but the police were called, and after a brief interrogation, JuJu "fessed up." Right after that, he circumvented the atrocity by promising to take summer employment with Pop Deleganes so he could pay for the damages.

Eddie, Dennis, Jeff, and I had already been on the job a couple weeks when JuJu was hired. Armed with 18–inch curved machetes, rounded on the tip and sharpened all the way around, we had been efficiently working our rows, hacking away some of the new growth to shape a fragrant pyramid. Awed by our newly–acquired weapons and their capacity for mayhem, however, we sometimes found it difficult to concentrate our "shaping" to fir trees, and by the time JuJu Perdicious started working with us, anything that stuck up above ground level was getting "pruned." Tall weeds, of course, were easy marks, but short weeds, toad stools, moths, and the occasional pine beetle got their share of action, too. When these were in short supply, we turned on each other, creeping up to playfully sever a suspender or disembowel a boot by slicing through the laces. Pop Deleganes tolerated these shenanigans for a time but put an emphatic, expletive–laced end to our fun after he had to rush Jeff to the emergency room where they sewed up a three–inch slice in his foot. "I can't baby–sit you heathens every minute," he said. "My insurance is killing me as it is! The next person to bleed on the job can start walking to town!"

Pop showed he was serious a couple days later by sending Jeff home unemployed after a careless follow–through sliced a sliver–thin piece of meat from his right thigh.

For a couple days, JuJu did pretty well. He wasn't the most coordinated guy in the world but he was persistent—you've got to admire him for trying. Then, he took on a night job flipping burgers at a highway burger joint and picked up a couple more hours as an early–morning fry cook in the same establishment. After a week of this, he was in bad shape—a walking zombie.

"Hey, JuJu," Eddie asked one soggy morning as the four us huddled in the relative dryness of the tool shed watching the rain form muddy puddles outside the doorway. "Does Pop know you're working three jobs?" JuJu didn't answer because he was sound asleep, hunkered there with his head on his knees. Eddie prodded him with an elbow. "Does he?" he repeated.

JuJu stirred and yawned. "Does he what?" he mumbled irritably, moving his head only slightly and talking into his knees.

"Does Pop know you're working those other jobs, too?" Eddie asked. "I thought there was some kind of law or somethin' against that."

JuJu's eyes were already red and watery, but he rubbed them vigorously with a balled–up fist. "I reckon I need the dough," he said. "I'm makin' payments on a ring for my girl, and my old man's bugging me about his car. If I don't work there's gonna be a whole lot of people waitin' to pull my hair out."

"Well, that ought to solve some of your problems," Eddie said brightly.

"Yeah," Dennis giggled. "And whadda *you* need a car for anyway? You ain't *never* gonna get yer license!"

Well, the pressure and the lack of sleep must have made JuJu irritable, because one thing led to another, and pretty soon he had Dennis by the shirt and was swinging him around inside the tool shed. Eddie and I then jumped into the fray on Dennis's side, and when Pop Deleganes drove up in his big green Dodge, we had ganged up on JuJu, drug him out into the rain, and were sitting on his head and back while he tried to snort obscenities through the mud in his nose. Pop quickly restored order to his Christmas tree plantation by threatening to fire the lot of us, but he directed an additional warning to JuJu. "Didn't have no trouble before you came." He growled and glowered, and the message was clear.

The rest of that day was uneventful, though Dennis, inspired by the support he had received, told about 3,000 bad–driver jokes, hollering them across his lane for everyone to hear. JuJu refused to be provoked, and even giggled a couple times. Probably, he was too tired to get mad. By quitting time, we had formed an uneasy truce under Pop's watchful eye.

The carnage began the next morning after Pop went to town. The four of us were doing okay, except JuJu seemed more tired than usual, shuffling around and stumbling in gopher holes. Then, came his first close call with a "springer."

The branches of our Douglas fir were extremely flexible. If one of us took a whack at the new growth and hit too far into the old, one of us was likely to be ducking a razor–bladed machete as it bounced back past his ear—a springer. If, on the other hand, the whack was too far forward to meet adequate resistance, the branch would "give," and the blade would continue through unimpeded to jeopardize the body's lower extremities. This, we called a "skive." I don't remember why. The first of JuJu's errant cuts was a "springer" that just missed his cheek. The second, witnessed by Jim, was a "skive" which ripped through his jeans but found no flesh. Perhaps there were others before the unlucky one that sliced into his knee.

"Ah *!&#@!" JuJu yelled from the end of his row.

"What?" I called.

"Ah *!&#@!" he repeated with just a little more whine. "I'm skived!"

JuJu was sitting on the ground with both hands clenched around his leg. Blood had already soaked through his Levi's. He was rocking back and forth.

"Does it hurt?" I asked, for lack of anything more conversational, but JuJu just grimaced and kept on rocking.

Eddie showed up. "Does it hurt?" he asked.

"I think it hurts," I said observantly. "That's why he's making those funny noises."

Then, Dennis came into the row. "That's gotta hurt!" he said as we watched a little trickle of blood escape from beneath the cuff of JuJu's jeans and dribble into his boot. "We better get him to the hospital."

"Yeah," Eddie agreed. "We better call an ambulance!"

JuJu shook his head. "Pop'll fire me!" he groaned. "I can't lose this job." His face was white. "You guys gotta bandage me up."

And that's what we did. Around the knee, Eddie wrapped some clean burlap strips and tied it off with baling twine. Except for the bulge, the blood on his pants, and the pronounced limp, JuJu was as good as new. Before long, he was listlessly pruning again.

The second accident came less than an hour later. This time, JuJu let out a howl, stumbling into my row with blood soaking through his shirt. A careless horizontal whack had sent his machete caroming into his sternum, scaring him as much as anything. "I'm hit! I'm hit!" he moaned dramatically. Underneath the shirt, an ugly six–inch slit was bleeding vigorously.

"It isn't very deep, JuJu," I said. "Pinch it together until I can get some more burlap and string." I started off at a jog, then turned. "You want to see a doctor?"

JuJu shook his head and looked down the road. "Is Pop back yet?" he moaned.

"Don't worry about Pop," I said. "Just stay out of sight when he gets here. He'll never find out."

In half an hour, I had JuJu on his feet and he insisted on going back to work. Blood now soaked his shirt and his right leg and was drying on his hands. He looked terrible, but not nearly so bad as he did a mere ten minutes later when a "springer" nearly severed his right ear.

There was no curse. There was no moan. Eddie, Dennis, and I were on the way back to the tool shed for lunch when JuJu stumbled into the road and just sort of stood there sway-

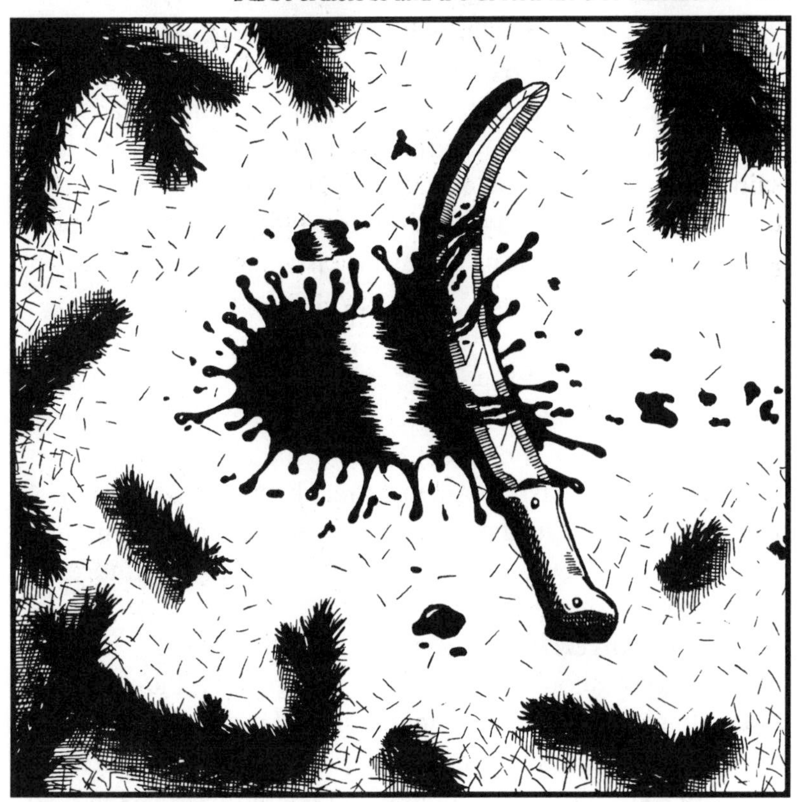

ing. He was in shock. "I think this is a bad one," he said almost calmly, the blood trickling down his cheek.

Cautiously, still wielding machetes, we approached our stricken comrade just as Pop Deleganes's Dodge wheeled around a turn and slid to a stop. Before him swayed the white–faced, red–eyed, utterly–bloodied figure of JuJu Perdicious surrounded by three armed assassins moving in to administer the coup de grace.

"Fer God's sake, don't!" Pop screamed as he threw himself between us. "Fer God's sake, you're ruining yer lives!" Pop had his arms outstretched downward and his palms open and he sort of bounced around like he was either playing defense for some grade school basketball team or trying to herd chickens through a narrow door.

Dennis was the first to perceive the misunderstanding, and the temptation overwhelmed him. "Let me at 'em! Let me at 'em!" he shrieked, raising his machete and dancing this way and that as Pop tried to counter his moves. Well, that got Eddie and I laughing, and pretty soon JuJu came out of his trance and he started laughing, too, though we couldn't imagine why, what with his ear hanging down alongside his cheek.

Finally, Pop figured out he'd jumped to a conclusion and missed. Folding his arms across his chest, he stepped back and looked JuJu up and down. "You having a bad day, son?" he asked.

"I'm havin' a bad life," JuJu said.

"I think they can sew that ear back on," Pop said sympathetically.

"That would make Bonnie Lee real happy," JuJu smiled.

Pop gently led JuJu over to the Dodge and tucked him in the back seat. "You fellas had lunch yet?" he asked kindly, turning to us.

"No sir, Mr. Deleganes sir," I answered politely.

"Well, you should," Pop said. "You should all go and take a nice, long lunch. Take an hour." He got in the car. "Heck," he said, his voice rising, "take two hours!" He slammed the door and rolled down the window. "Take the whole dang day!" he said, spit flying like little white bullets from his lips as the red crept higher up his face. "But don't you never, never, tell anybody what happened out here today!"

And I never did.

Until now.

All about stress

It is becoming increasingly popular these days to blame ugly, stupid, or even pernicious deeds on stress, a natural reaction of the body to a demand. The medical community, though admitting stress is something we create ourselves rather than something "out there," has still published lists of "symptoms" that could indicate too much stress. Included are such subtle tip–offs as clenched fists, chain smoking, and a desire to put Kibbles and Bits between your toes before dressing for work. By studying the medical lists, however, the individual with the misplaced Kibbles and Bits will not have to say, "Gee, I must be weird!" No, he can say, "Gee, I must be stressed. No doubt this also justifies my need to spit on small animals and maim my body by putting pierced jewelry in places my mother always told me not to touch."

I know for a fact that bird hunting can be stressful. Physical demands such as getting up in the dark to chase a turkey, or removing porcupine quills from a hundred–pound Labrador, would most definitely be considered stressors, though the psychological demands of hunting are even greater. Psychological demands, the experts tell me, are things like worry and embarrassment and deadlines. If I worry about whether to hunt pheasants first and take a chance of someone beating me to the quail covey in Eva's Pasture, I am, by definition, stressed. If I am embarrassed by my shooting and the performance of my dogs (and I am), I am stressed. If I wonder about the consequences of missing Lacey's six o' clock dinner party because the doves are flying, I am stressed. Not only that, I will not be offered a late meal when I get home and will probably be asked to sleep alone in the guest room besides. That will generate additional stress. The good part, though, is that all this stress may give me leave to commit an eccentric and socially unacceptable act without fear of any real punishment. If, for example, I should decide to sabotage the swarms of mosquito–like jet skis that have invaded the once–peaceful bays of Loon Lake, I will most likely receive little more than a "naughty, naughty" from the local courts. If burglary and extortion bring only a couple days in the slammer, putting sand in the gas tank of a jet ski can't be worth much more than a nose tweak. Using stress as my defense, I can probably even find someone to sue.

All–in–all, the medical profession has given us over 50 symptoms indicative of stress. These include overeating, diarrhea, mouth noises, leg wagging, sleeping too much, distractability, proneness to errors, confusion, nightmares, indigestion, skin problems, a desire to run away, and an inability to talk. With this as a guideline, I have determined that both my Lab and my springer are suffering from perpetual stress. However, as the medical gurus remind me, "What is stressful for one is not necessarily stressful for all," and doggy stress is darn near impossible to identify. Possibly, Dude and Sundy get worked up about things that don't concern me a bit—like what movie star is dating what counter–culture icon with ties to the kitty–art movement, or whether or not Senator Wackwood's mother sleeps in a Velcro nighty. For darn sure my dogs don't worry about staying in range, flatulence, or soft retrieves.

Now that I have determined that both my dogs and I suffer from stress, I would like to do something about it. To make this easier, the local hospital where I am on a first–name basis with the emergency room staff, has sent me a "Wellness" pamphlet that lists 52 proven stress reducers. Suggestion number one is that I "prepare for the morning the evening before." I guess this means that if I have a grouse hunt planned for the a.m., I should get my boots and my sandwiches good and wet that night, bark my shins a couple times, put five miles on my treadmill, and take the dogs out and hide them where I won't see them again until lunch time. The pamphlet also says, "Don't put up with something that doesn't work right," but if I follow *that* advice, I'll have to get rid of my own body and I'm not done with it yet. Some parts of me are showing signs of wear, but as far as I know, they're the only parts I'm going to be issued.

There are many other proven stress reducers mentioned in my pamphlet from the hospital. These include, "Don't rely on your memory." (Whose, then?) "Do nothing which leads you to lie." (Stop fishing and hunting?) "Practice preventive maintenance." (Don't let the kids drive the car?) "Eliminate the amount of caffeine in your diet." (I'd rather die!) "Create order out of chaos." (Leave my storage shed out of this!) and, "Every day do something you enjoy." (Sure. But what will I do about February and March)?

My favorite medically–endorsed, stress–reducing ploy is number 39 which says, "Do something that will improve your appearance." Since face transplants have not yet been perfected and brown paper bags are not always handy, I must assume this means I should upgrade my outdoor apparel. I think new boots, a new vest, and a nice pair of brush pants would keep stress at bay at least as long as number 51 which says I should accept the fact I live in an imperfect world.

Camping with the arrow

"Sir," he said, "did you know you came in against the arrow?"

I leaned out my car window to look where he indicated. "What arrow might that be?" I asked.

"The big yellow one painted on the asphalt there," he said, indicating a big yellow one painted on the asphalt. "If you wish to camp in a national park, sir, you must abide by the rules."

"Sorry," I said. "Am I under arrest?"

The youthful ranger pushed his Smokey hat back on his head and scrutinized me from behind yellow–tinted sun glasses. Then he grunted. "Not just yet, sir, but we would certainly appreciate your cooperation here at Misty River National Park. Violators will not be tolerated."

"I'm trying to quit," I said. Just ahead, in campsight #1, I watched a red–faced man in fluorescent Bermuda shorts strain to adjust the TV antenna atop a 45–foot trailer. Somewhere in the bowels of his silver and yellow getaway, his wife and children were "roughing it" with a Fred Flintstone rerun. A small, white dog that looked like a rat with hyperthyroidism pushed his head out a window and growled at me, so I batted the air and hissed like an angry mountain lion. When he leapt back to safety with a yip, I chuckled. "But tell me, son," I said, remembering the ranger, "is this a good place to camp?"

The sun glasses caught my reflection as he leaned out the window of his little booth. "What you just did there," he said with a frown, "was extremely antisocial. Animal companions are most welcome here as long as they are well–mannered."

"Sorry. Really," I said. "But what about it? Other than the 'yabba dabba doos' coming from that traveling hotel over there, is this a good place to camp?"

"The woods are lovely, dark and deep," the ranger said softly.

"Frost?" I asked.

"Not for another month or so," he answered seriously. "Once in a while it rains this time of year, but it won't get that cold."

A commotion to the left caught my attention and I looked out the window again just as a chipmunk wearing a yellow plastic radio transistor sped across the road. In close pursuit were approximately 300 children on skate boards, each with a dog. "Shouldn't they be on a leash?" I asked.

"Why, yes they should," the ranger affirmed, leaning far out to evaluate the situation. "And it appears they are." He strained just a little further. "Every canine companion appears to be properly restrained," he said happily. "Per park policy."

"I was talking about the kids," I said, "but never mind. Guess I'll just mosey on down toward the water and look for a spot to throw my bag. I've been driving solid for two days, and I'm looking forward to holing up for awhile."

"Take these with you," the ranger said, handing me a stack of brochures. "You may have campsite 206. I'm sure you will find the accommodations lovely. The pay showers are to your right, the recreation hall to the left. There will be a nature walk after lunch, and don't forget the evening amphitheater program." He smiled and held out his hand. "That will be 12 dollars, please."

"Twelve dollars!" I exclaimed. "Just to throw down a sleeping bag?"

"In a designated camping spot only, of course," he said.

"You got anything for $2.50?" I asked. "I'm a little short. My vacation lasted longer than I'd anticipated, see. . . ."

The ranger shook his head slowly from side to side. "The fee is twelve dollars," he said. "Believe me, sir, it's worth it. The amphitheater program alone is worth the money."

"Well, how 'bout I just stay in my sleeping bag, forget about taking a shower, and let someone have my place in the recreation hall?" I asked. "I really just want to sleep about 12 hours and be on my way again." I knew that I, the man who had once set a North American record by going an entire summer in Alaska without formally washing, would not miss a little warm water now. And though my crustiness then had more to do with economics, the high cost of mosquito dope, and the fact I went on a three month fishing frenzy during which I lost all track of time, place, and social civility, it certainly wouldn't hurt to save a couple quarters at this juncture, either.

"Twelve dollars," the ranger repeated. "This is not a negotiable item, sir."

"Alright, alright," I grumbled, digging out my last fifteen dollars. "Does 206 have a fire pit? Looks like I'll be eating hotdogs again tonight."

"Fires are not allowed here, sir," the ranger said. "If you

wish, you may purchase a burrito at the snack bar, however. Use of the microwave is free."

"Microwave?" I blurted incredulously. "Microwave! What happened to good old burnt weinies and sooty beans? What about the wood smoke and the bug spray and the paper plate that gets all soggy and falls apart even before the watermelon? You call this camping, mister?"

Granted, I had not camped in a national park for many years, but what was a camping trip without the charred food? What was camping without the unidentifiable sounds in the night that made you hold your breath at the bottom of your sleeping bag? What use was a good comic book or scary novel without a dying flashlight, dancing shadows on the wall of a canvas tent, and the musty smell of freedom and adventure? Had camping, also, been sanitized, regulated, and made so utterly bland it had become a pathetic extension of what man had hoped to escape when he first determined to leave his home in town and pitch a tent among the trees?

"Our other guests haven't complained," he said. "Misty River has an excellent reputation."

"Oh?" I said, quickly thumbing through a brochure. "Is that based on your gourmet burritoes or the accuracy of your marked nature trails?" I thumbed a little further. "Perhaps it's the quality of your pine needle baskets. It says here you employ some of the area's finest artisans to teach the class."

"That is correct," he said smugly. "And don't forget the fish–smoking demonstration or the porcupine quill art. We use liquid smoke and simulated quills. Why, some of our campers are here just to take the advanced leathercraft classes." He smiled. "Imitation leather, of course."

"Mister," I finally said, "all I want to do is sleep. Point me toward 206 and I won't bother you any more."

"Will you be wanting a wake–up call?" he asked. "There's a delightful wild flower seminar right after the nature walk."

"Thank you, but that won't be necessary," I assured him. "I'll probably wander down to the aerobics class on the beach and degrade myself instead." I looked at the schedule. "That's not until late afternoon, however. I'll certainly be awake by then."

"Excellent choice, sir!" he said. "Excellent choice indeed. But do be careful to take the correct trail. Two roads diverge in the woods. . . ."

"Frost?" I asked again, hopefully.

"Chance of rain," he said. "Haven't we been through this already?"

"Sorry," I said. "I guess we have." I started my car, lurched forward, and killed it as a bewhiskered man in a late–model truck pulled into the spot I had vacated.

"Sir," I heard the young ranger say to him, "did you know you came in against the arrow?"

The wild game banquet

Many years ago, one of my hunting buddies completed a triple on blue grouse on a ridge above Deer Lake. Mike was so overwhelmed with this miracle, he shot three rolls of film and sent some of the pictures to a local outdoor tabloid. When they were published, he took a lot of razzing from the rest of us as we had never before seen a grouse trussed to the hood of a car, but Mike said he wasn't about to let the most momentous day in his bird hunting life go unnoticed. Furthermore, he said, we were all invited to his house to partake of the bounty of his success. That, our first wild game banquet, was the beginning of a tradition.

Around our own homes, I, and most of my hunting and fishing friends, are adequate cooks at best, but each year the wild game banquet brought out the gourmet in us all. After the feast, we would sit around the kitchen table sipping Eddie's homemade huckleberry hooch, smoking big cigars, and contemplating the destruction we had wrought upon platters of crab–stuffed pheasant breasts, mallard in orange sauce, and barbecued elk backstrap. Sometimes during this after–dinner hiatus, the conversation turned to politics or foreign policy, but most often we dwelt on important philosophical issues like whether a recently–purchased fly rod actually existed if the purchaser was still hiding it from his wife.

I'm not certain when our dinners began to deteriorate, but Mike says it was '86 when Eddie brought the magpie quiche. Eddie, of course, refuses to accept the blame and maintains he didn't bring the quiche until '88—the year after Tom served the porcupine meatloaf. Tom says that was different, as we all knew it was porcupine meatloaf, but passing off magpies as grouse was a dirty trick. Personally, I thought Eddie's creation was delicious, though listening to Steve wretch in the bathroom after dinner detracted from its enjoyment.

Gradually, things just got out of hand. Our wild game banquet became a contest to see who could prepare and disguise the most unlikely dish. Our dinners deteriorated from exotic to questionable to disgusting, from bear roast and mountain sheep steak through beaver tail, muskrat, and starfish soup. Even when one of us would bring a more traditional offering of pheasant Kiev or baked sockeye in dill sauce, the others would sniff and probe it suspiciously, fearful of being "got." It was one thing to consume minute proportions of carp or a raven casserole, but none of us wanted to swallow a large portion of "marinated moose brisket" and later learn there was a ground squirrel pattering around in our stomachs.

In 1993, Mike, who is a taxidermist and has access to all sorts of unusual creatures, brought cougar steaks and passed them off as ruffed grouse. The meat was white, finely textured, and cut to the exact dimensions of filleted grouse breasts. Thankful to have something to eat that we recognized, Tom, Eddie, Steve, and I dug in. It was delicious. Mike helped himself to salads, sampled my mussel stew, and poked around in a questionable, dark–meated casserole Eddie insisted contained Canada goose. But he didn't sample the "grouse." It was not until well into our after–dinner cigars that he pushed back his chair, grinned fiendishly, and began pawing at the air, spitting and hissing like a treed tom, suggesting the birch trees in the back yard were climbable if the dog was making any of us nervous. With considerable mirth, he then revealed the nature of what we had gluttonously consumed, and howled with laughter as Eddie and I turned green, Steve headed for the bathroom, and Tom sat staring vacantly at the tablecloth, his lips pursed and cheeks bulging.

Much later, after Eddie quit meowing, we made a pact. Our wild game banquet had begun as a celebration of friendship and good fortune afield, and we all agreed that was what it should again become. In the years to follow, there would be no barbecued coyote ribs, no poached salamander. Mike went to get another round of cigars, and Steve poured another round of huckleberry hooch in preparation of a toast to good fishing, good hunting, and good friends. Just to even things out, however, he dropped his false teeth into Mike's glass.

A knotty problem

Actually, there is nothing really wrong with the granny—a very basic knot fashioned just prior to the first loop in shoe–tieing. Were it not the first learned, it would be more popular today, but there is something about growing up that causes many of us to forsake simple but effective things in pursuit of sophistication, and there is nothing simpler than a granny.

Despite its provinciality, I always found the granny knot useful, and its offspring, the double granny, would secure anything that needed securing. Nevertheless, the sportsman who tethers his horse on wilderness pack trips or ties on a clown pattern Spin 'n Glo for king salmon with a double granny, had best be prepared for callous ridicule from associates and guides.

"What the hell is this mess?" my friend, Herb Ladding, grunted as we broke camp in Idaho's Nez Perce National Forest. It had been my first elk hunt and we had both shot respectable bulls by the third morning out. Herb was in the process of taking down the tent while I rolled up the sleeping bags. The "mess" he referred to was a series of double grannies I had used to secure our four–man wall tent to the surrounding forest.

"A double granny," I replied without embarrassment.

"A double granny!" Herb repeated incredulously. "Now you don't say? I haven't seen a granny since I earned my Bobcat badge for Den 14 back in '53. Ever hear of a double half hitch? What about a slip knot? Surely you're familiar with that one."

"Huh–uh." I was beginning to feel inadequate, and my neck was getting hot, so employing a proven personal theory that a vigorous attack is superior to any type of retreat, I rose to my feet. "You got complaints about the way I put up the tent, Herb? Maybe you didn't notice we had a pretty good wind last night. Did you have to come out in your underwear and tie down the tent? Huh?"

Herb stared at me, then shook his head slowly and clucked his tongue. "That's got nothing to do with it at all," he said. "What if some of the boys from the next camp had seen these knots? You ever think about that? Do you think they would have still offered to help pack out those elk? Do you think they would have asked us to sit in on their poker games?"

"Well, why wouldn't they?" I asked. "What's a knot got to do with anything?"

Herb spat. "Experience," he said with annoyance, wiping his hand quickly across his face. "Experience. You think they'd have extended the same courtesies to a couple greenhorns? Not on your life!" He moved slowly away from the tent as he spoke, and I was sure he was about to continue his oratory from atop a nearby stump. "A man's got to earn the respect of his neighbors out here," he continued, "and there isn't a soul on this mountain that wouldn't have labeled us dudes if they'd seen those knots you tied. They would have left us all by our lonesome and we'd still be packing the hindquarters."

Herb glared at me for a few moments, strolled back to the tent, and began slashing at the ropes with his skinning knife. Kneeling again to his sleeping bag, I added another granny to the two already securing it and cinched them all down harder than necessary. Stalemate. Still, I couldn't help but wonder if perhaps it was time I developed some sophistication in my knot–tying.

Back home a few days later, I walked to the library and checked out a full set of old Cub Scout handbooks and a manual put out by a fishing tackle manufacturer. In a matter of hours, I had mastered the blood knot, but try as I might, could not get the hang of the bowline, the overhand, or the square bow knot. For one thing, the diagrams appeared to be upside down, and for another, I could not differentiate between the drawing of the twine and the drawings of the arrows that showed me what to do with the twine. Every time I doubled the length, looped the middle, ran one end through the loop and the other around it, then pulled—presto—the knot disappeared.

After lunch, I tried again, this time with the book held flat open on the floor, weighted down with an ashtray and a fireplace poker while I hovered above and behind. This method seemed to put the diagrams into perspective, and after a few false starts during which I somehow secured the thumb and forefinger on my left hand to the middle of my right, I was able to loop and pull my two–foot length of practice cord into either a half hitch, a slip knot, or a sheep's bend. I wasn't sure which, but the trick lay in not trying to predict the outcome. It was far more effective to wait until the knot materialized and then study the pages of diagrams to see what I had tied.

Thus, having finally achieved a level of mediocrity in about 12 hours, I took the next day off, loaded the boat, and set off for some steelhead fishing on the Snake River. There I discovered that a rather painless procedure with a short cord in the living room was a whole different can of worms with a 20–foot length of rope, a heaving dock, and an 18–foot inboard that needed to be secured in a squall. It was one thing to be able to hold both ends of a two–foot cord in my hands while practicing the double hitch, and quite another when trying to tie the same knot when one end was fastened to the bow of a heaving boat and the excess was wrapped around my legs. When the primary consideration became "Get the job done and get the hell out of the rain," guess which knot was the only one remembered? The granny, of course. Two of them.

By its nature, knot tying is a skill that should be reinforced on a daily basis, and this creates a dilemma. Outside of weekend forays in the pursuit of fish and game, 20th century man does not often have the need to tie most knots. As a result, they are forgotten. Tying is not a skill on which he is likely to be tested in the course of his employment as an accountant or computer programmer. When the boss comes into the office and tells me to organize the Higbley file and get it in the mail pronto, I do not ask her if she wants it secured with a Palomar or a sheepshank.

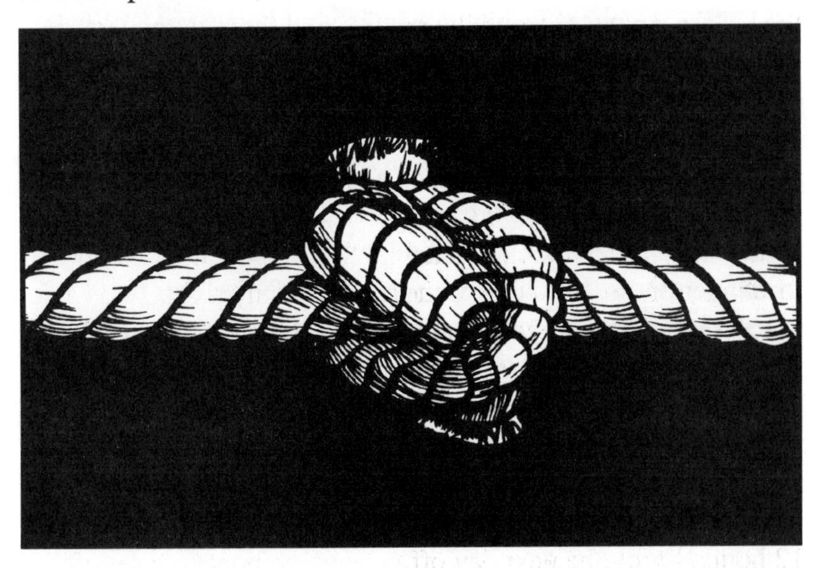

Despite my difficulties, I continued to study knots. I really did want to impress Herb on our next big game hunt. That summer, I used the blood knot for tying on all my fishing lures, and I also developed a pretty fair half hitch, but then I discovered a novel, inexpensive device called an elastic shock cord that made packing for weekend campouts with my family a pleasure and almost eliminated the need for all but angling knots. Given enough shock cord, I could fasten every possession in the house and garage to my camper. Surely, I decided, even Herb would not complain if I brought a few of these wonderful lengths of elastic to our hunting camp, and with that determination, I quickly forgot everything I had almost learned. A dry run in the backyard had proven that with shock cords I could even erect a tent in half the time it ordinarily took.

Imagine my disappointment that fall when Herb and I

arrived at our camping spot, unloaded our gear, and discovered one duffel missing. Closing my eyes, I could see it waiting expectantly but forgotten in the corner of the garage.

"What'd you have in that thing, anyway?" Herb chuckled. "The way you're acting, you'd think it was your jammies." He shoved his toe against a green canvas duffel. "I saw 'em in here with your sleeping bag and Teddy bear," he said, "and over there is your rifle, and in here is your heavy coat. What else do you need?"

"I guess it wasn't that important, Herb," I sighed. "You want me to dig the latrine and cut some wood?"

"Naw, I'll do that," he said. "You pitch the tent."

Reluctantly, I began what had evidently become my traditional camp chore, and try as I might, I could remember none of the diagrams from my Cub Scout handbooks. For the second year in a row, our four–man wall tent went up, secured to trees and underbrush with the inferior double granny. When I finished, I sat on a stump and fiddled with the gas stove, dreading Herb's discovery and appraisal of my work.

"What the hell is this?" he asked me a short time later. Like a replay from the year before, he was fingering the knots I had tied.

I know not the sudden source of my inspiration, but without hesitation, I answered. "It's called a triple Ferguson with a sliding glitch. I used it in 'Nam to tie down Hueys."

Herb patted my double granny affectionately with the back of his hand and smiled. "Now *that's* a knot," he said, and walked away whistling.

Navigating by moss

I worry about it. My friends and family joke about it. It has caused me no small amount of embarrassment: my sense of direction is non–existent.

I am the only man in the world who has to backtrack to find the front door after taking out the garbage. My wife makes me carry a flare gun when I go for a walk with the dog, and way back in the first grade, I gained some permanent notoriety with my peers, my principal, and my parents by walking six full miles home from school following the first day of classes in September. Had we not lived at the end of the block the school was on, this would have been a heroic trek for one so young. When Dad finally found me, I was approaching the city limits on the opposite side of town and had just about decided my folks had moved—house and all—while I was breathing the oppressive air in Miss Rodney's room.

For an adult, getting lost epitomizes the word "embarrassment." Most men, in fact, will admit only to "getting separated from the party" or "becoming disoriented." At the time of occurrence they fear they will never again see a familiar face, but this is nothing compared to the mortification of admitting to a need to be rescued; *that* does things to the ego. Lost hunters and fishermen and hikers and bird watchers could spare themselves considerable grief if they would put this false pride aside and holler like hell for help. That's what *I* should have done last fall when I became seriously separated from my three deer hunting buddies, but fearing ridicule, I forged onward. Surely, I could work it out myself.

In half a minute, I had leveled a 200–yard swath of willow in a blind, panic–induced sprint. Had a large spruce not

jumped in front of me, I would have probably mowed down additional vegetation. Knocked to the ground, I sucked in great bucketsful of forest–scented oxygen and got a grip on myself—a two–handed throat hold with the thumb pressed against a critical pressure point. I had learned this move years before as a method of getting out of bad situations, when I attempted for a year to teach elementary education, which is a *really* bad situation. My principal, though, had made me quit using it on myself because the kids got scared when I passed out.

Once I had calmed down some and my fingers relaxed, I began to assay my predicament in a slightly more rational manner. Soon, I remembered a bit of botanical trivia I felt might be useful. Years before, someone had told me moss grew on the north side of trees. I think this was the same individual who told me he knew where street lights went when they died, but jumping up, I nevertheless tried to substantiate this postulate. My conclusions, though, were unsatisfactory. While there *did* seem to be more moss on one side of each tree that was inclined to grow it, some had no tendency for mossiness at all, and even were I able to establish north from south, what good would it have done me anyway? Navigating by moss would be haphazard at best. I knew my mother was hosting her annual autumn tea that day in the shade of the north side of her home, but I doubted that following mossy trees would enable me to get there before the finger sandwiches were gone.

Next, I remembered the running water theory. Every outdoorsman has learned that small creeks feed into larger streams which flow into still larger rivers, which empty into oceans, but no one ever mentioned *which* ocean. I figured if I followed the creek I was near, there was a 50–50 chance I'd hit Cape Hateras on the Atlantic, which was about 5,000 miles further than I wanted to go. Then, when I finally stumbled to the car years later, everyone would think I had been lost. Heaven forbid!

It was while culling this possibility and mulling over others, that I recalled a deer hunting tradition I thought might allow me to save the day and face. If we have separated to hunt, it is customary for my group of buddies to meet somewhere at noon to eat lunches, compare notes, and stretch a truth or two. We are always ready to sit down together on a sunny south slope, relax, drink Mike's thermos of coffee, and devour the home–made donuts Lacey always contributes to the outing.

Stepping to the top of the highest deadfall in sight, I cupped my hands around my mouth, leaned back, and bellowed for all I was worth: 'Donnnuttts!' Never had there been a louder and more seductive call to lunch.

When the echoes had a last been absorbed by brush and stone, I quit breathing to listen. Far below me, someone—probably Mike—took up the call and passed it along to the others. Joyfully, I bounded down hill toward the sound of his voice, and before long, could see the glint of sunlight on rifle barrel. I'd take a razzing for making the call so early, but so what if it was only 10:30? A faulty timepiece is a lot easier to explain than becoming disoriented.

Ms. Oglethorpe–Ross, Editor
Birds of a Feather Magazine
PO Box 2, Suite 3
Mawn, PA

Dear Ms. Hyphen:

Well, I imagine I've been fired. It's not something I'm used to, but no one but myself should feel bad about it. Ma'am, I'm awful sorry about the waterfowl pictures I promised and didn't deliver in time for your last issue. Given the amount of time I spent in that blind this winter, I should have easily fulfilled your photo requests.

I'd plead ignorant, but my father, whom I greatly admired, used to say, "Ignorance excuses no man." My father, you must understand, did all things in moderation, which minimized the opportunities to look stupid; I am prone to excess. Dad also used to say, "Rashness excuses no man, No man is an island, Save your empties," and "Read the directions." He liked to cover all the bases. I spent a good part of my youth, in fact, trying without success to find a base he hadn't covered. Dad even knew a little bit about the relationships between cellulose digestion, methane gas, and the rumen. I'm not sure what base that covered, though. Do you?

But enough about my father. I was attempting to explain why I did not get the cover shot and the inside verticals you requested for your article on puddle ducks. The fact is, I was so certain my new $800 camera would make me an artist, I overlooked some basic strategies for good photography—like putting in film and taking off the lens cap. I blew several photo opportunities with those oversights, Ms. Hyphen, but my biggest obstacle was the salesman who convinced me my camera had a mind of its own—that I had to but show up and it would begin creating Kodak Moments. In all fairness, he *did* tell me to get to know my equipment. He wasn't very specific, however. My camera and I barbecued turkey hotdogs one afternoon and enjoyed a couple long early–morning walks around the lake. Perhaps that wasn't adequate. Perhaps we should have talked, got in touch with our inner selves. Maybe I should have served all–beef franks instead of the turkey.

Who am I kidding, Ms. Hyphen? It was not the salesman's fault, it was mine—and not just because I didn't read the operator's manual. I proved something to myself last December and January that I had suspected all along: I am a hunter. You remember, of course, that thousand dollar cover shot you wanted—three mallards, stacked in a descending V with their wings set. You said you wanted the birds to fill the frame, with nothing but water in the background. You said you wanted your readers to "hear the downdraft." Well, I took that shot, Ms. Hyphen—with my 12–gauge. Couldn't help it. When I saw those ducks lock up right over the decoys, I dropped the camera and grabbed the gun. The same thing happened with the drake pintail over the top of the corn stubble. He was right there where you wanted him, but when I sat up to click off a couple shots, my shotgun was in my hands and my camera was nowhere to be found.

I know you're thinking I didn't make much of an effort at picture–taking. I know you're thinking a serious photographer would have left his shotgun at home. Well, I did, Ms. Hyphen—I left it at home the very next trip. It wasn't that hard, as I've had plenty of practice during the off–season. Lots of times in March and April, I have enjoyed driving out to the blind and just sitting there watching those birds go about the business of living. A duck is a pretty amazing creature, Ms. Hyphen, pretty amazing indeed. Admirable, even. Sometimes, I have taken Lacey or one of the kids. Once, after watching a group of mallards in their twisting, whimsical, courting flights, my niece, Janie, asked me if ducks knew how great they were. Pretty perceptive for an eight–year–old, wouldn't you say?

But this wasn't the off–season. You'll probably never understand the feeling that came over me, huddled there in full camouflage during legal shooting hours, surrounded by ducks. A camera, Ms. Hyphen? It was blasphemy. During the duck season, a duck–hunting man hunts ducks. When the first pair set their wings and started to drop into my decoys, I stood up and threw my camera!

I guess I won't be asking for any more photo assignments, ma'am. I'm not cut out for wildlife photography, and anyway, it will be quite a while before I can afford another camera. I've been thinking seriously about going back to a $12 instamatic or maybe even one of those disposable jobs that shoot under water—which is where I find myself on occasion. Despite your opinion of me, I *do* need a camera. I'm not real big on "after the hunt" shots, either, but I like to keep a scrapbook of dogs and blinds and the men who share my memories. Ma'am—I do hope you find the right photographer for next year. You might try my cousin, Izzak. He doesn't hunt a lick.

Best wishes,

Alan Liere

Alan Liere

It's about time

Having recently returned from my first chukar hunt of the year, and having nothing better to do while waiting for the inflammation in my knees and ankles to subside, I entered into some rather haphazard ruminations of the things I don't understand, which are a lot. Some, of course, like yogurt and tofu will never make sense to me because I don't want them to. Others, like megabytes, modem, and modifier keys, I pursue reluctantly through the dust of technology for no other reason except I like to be miserable. Misery builds character, and nothing makes me more miserable than calling myself stupid and trying to figure out how much RAM I need for virtual memory on my 80 MB Quantum.

What with all the new electronic safety and anti–pollution devices, I hardly know enough anymore to start my lawn mower. I bribed my pre–teenage niece, Janie, to program the timer on my sprinkling system, but I had to wait a week to view my new dog training video because the VCR is user hostile and my wife, who is our official "VCR Person," had taken Janie with her to visit friends down in Oregon. The same week, my pickup told me via a flashing red light that it was in need of maintenance, but when I took it to my mechanic, he told me via a bill for 22 dollars that the truck was just "goofing off." The next day, however, I discovered that when the low fuel indicator light comes on, it means business; I had to walk four miles for gas, but what really ticked me off was I missed the evening flight of doves in Doc Rainey's stubble field.

There are, of course, a lot of other things I don't understand, but I think I'm finally beginning to make some sense of time. For decades, I have puzzled over seconds, minutes, days, weeks, centuries, and February. I believe I heard one time that the ancient Mayan Indians had something to do with all those, but then again, maybe they were the ones who invented maize and line dancing, and it was the Romans who decided our second month would be short and boring. I also suspect the Latins, whoever they were, were mixed up in this. In any event, I think it absolutely fascinating that prior to my birth, some ancient individual, perhaps even Bob Hope, determined a week would always be seven days long with either five days at the beginning and two at the end, or one at the beginning, one at the end, and five in the middle, depending on which church you attend. Think how confusing and inconvenient it would be if a week had four more days! What would they be called? The good names are already used up. Would any of these extra days be included in the weekend? If I mowed my lawn once a week in an 11–day week, the weeds would be two feet high. And what about bird hunting? It is foolish to think one could go longer than seven days without a shotgun and a dog and a long walk through autumn finery, and seven is the perfect number needed for recovery from that same walk. On day five I'm still too sore, but on day six, I'm beginning to remember the good parts, and by day seven, I've forgotten everything but close flushes and fantastic shots. My only complaint about weeks, anymore, is that those of the vacation persuasion are far shorter than the others.

Seconds, minutes, and hours, I can see now, are also of perfect duration. "Wait a second" would be a rude demand if a second lasted longer than it does. The same with minutes. Consider, too, the dissention caused if an hour spanned the full cycle of the moon, as in "Honey, I'll be home in two hours." As a child, I was locked in a room and forced to practice the piano for an hour each day, but in those days, an hour in "the music room" *did* last the full cycle of the moon, especially if my friends were fishing down on Chimmikain Creek.

A year, as best I can determine, spans the sum of the days of the months within that year. This is neither new math nor original thinking, and you can check my veracity by counting on your calendar. If you clench your left hand into a fist with the fingers down and begin counting the knuckles and valleys from right to left beginning with January on the first knuckle and coming back to that knuckle for August, your friends will probably leave the room. You will discover, however, that the knuckle months all have 31 days and the valleys have 30, except for February, which has 28 or 29, depending on what church you attend. If this is too difficult, you might want to memorize the old stand–by, "Thirty days has September, June, July, and Remember. All the rest have 32 except February during which there's nothing to do." Or something like that. The main thing to remember about years is they go by very slowly when you are a youngster and much too quickly once you hit 40, which I did a decade or so ago, but it seems like only yesterday.

Get yer chukar?

My wife, Lacey, has noticed I don't not hunt chukars as much as I used to. She insists that at one time, I'd take three or four legitimate chukar trips a year, and by the end of the season, those three or four had become seven or eight. By mid–February, she says, I was up to 12, and anyone talking to me in June, would think I had camped September to January on the Snake River breaks and chased partridge every day. I was a legend in my own mind because my ability to disremember was more acute than anyone's.

I'm not yet in my "veranda years," but I don't mind admitting anymore that three or four chukar hunts per season are ample. To tell the truth, even thinking about more than that puts my charley horses into a canter and gives me blisters and cotton mouth. The last couple years, I have considered permanently forsaking the sport because my recovery time has eaten up opportunities to hunt quail and pheasant and ducks and dove and three varieties of grouse. Once, I spent an entire week in bed with an unhappy intestinal parasite because, in the course of a chukar hunt, I drank my canteen dry, and rather than go home, elected to share a warm–water spring with a herd of extremely unsanitary range cattle.

There is a problem with giving up chukar hunting: I, like thousands of other sportsmen, have come to use the activity as a mental elixir against creeping old age. In his own mind, a man who can still hunt chukars has assured himself of many autumns to come. Miss a year voluntarily, and who knows? Instant senility, hairy knuckles, and liver spots. I can't take chances with that sort of stuff. No one can. It's bad enough that my hair line and my physique have begun to migrate; I don't wish to encourage a mass exodus. The challenge, then, is to reduce the number of hunts I must make to insure peace of mind.

A friend of mine, Skip Hensler, was already an ex–chukar gunner when, in a lottery–type drawing, he won a big horn sheep permit on the Washington state side of Hell's Canyon. A former paratrooper, Skip, at fifty–something years of age, was in pretty good shape for a man who had spent more time in a car and at a desk than he liked to think about, but he quickly and painfully discovered he was no match for Hell's Canyon in September. Probably, he was no match for Hell's Canyon anytime. Despite his rigorous, hurry–up reconditioning regime, the black basalt cliffs, treacherous talus slides, and parched, rattlesnake–infested landscape of this prime chukar country convinced Skip that desire will not always compensate for physical maintenance, and that there are times when one would trade a loving wife for a sip of cold water. After three days of indescribable misery, he limped home with his tattered boots in his hands.

Rich Landers, a local outdoor editor interviewed Skip right after he returned from his ordeal. In an attempt to make him feel better, Rich reminded Skip that because he didn't shoot a ram, he could apply for the lottery again in five years. "Maybe next time you'll better know how to prepare yourself," he suggested.

Skip looked at Rich uncomfortably and shook his head. "But I *did* shoot a ram," he told him. "A little half–curl about a hundred yards from the river. Took him on the way out. The meat is wonderful, but once you fill your tag, you can *never* put in for another sheep hunt. I wanted to make sure I wasn't tempted."

I got to thinking about Skip's experience and what he did, and it occurred to me that perhaps a similar law could be applied to chukar hunting. With the stroke of a pen, the Department of Fish and Wildlife could change the status of this red–legged partridge (some word that would suggest they were either in short supply or likely to be. "Compromised" sounds adequately vague) and determine that henceforth, anyone over 45 would be allowed to shoot but one chukar *for the rest of his life.* In doing so, they would ingratiate themselves to the aging chukar gunners of the world and still assure hunting privileges to youngsters too green to feel pain.

First Aging Hunter: "Get yer chukar?"

Second Aging Hunter: "Sure did! Packed in and camped in that Big Spring Canyon the other side of Steptoe. Heard them on the second morning but didn't put one in the bag for two more days after that."

First Aging Hunter: "A good one?"

Second Aging Hunter: "Probably won't make the book, but he was prime. No pin feathers and dressed out at about three–quarters pound. What about you?"

First Aging Hunter: "Got mine last year. A nice bird. Had him mounted. Guess that's it for both of us. Too bad, huh?"

Both Aging Hunters smile broadly, wink, and go happily about their quail hunting.

Slide, please

With the holiday season closing in and the whole famdamnily coming to our house for Christmas day, I have been putting together another of my famous and incredibly perceptive slide shows. There is nothing so traditional at our family get–togethers as hauling out the old projector, hanging a sheet on the living room wall, turning off the lights, and reviewing my year afield.

Now, I know what you are saying; I know you are saying, "Yechhh!" or "Ughhh!" or "Count me out." I know this because I, too, have set through countless hours of home slide shows wherein Uncle Willard from Rathdrum showed 5,000 slides of Aunt Twila feeding the water buffalo at the W. P. Hermiston Memorial Dangerous Mammal and Endangered Amphibian Exhibit in Claybur, Idaho, concluding each image with a chuckle while pointing out that "Twila is the one on the right."

Yes, I am forever appalled at the dearth of quality and depth exhibited in the photographic endeavors of relatives and friends. But *my* slide shows are not like that. I have never taken a bad picture, and my presentations combine perfect images with artistic sensitivity. But why am I *telling* you all this? Sit back, friend. I'll turn off the light there, and you can see for yourself. Tell you what. . . You run the projector and I'll just stand up here with the pointer. Ready then? Okay. Slide, please.

Okay. This is Uncle Wil. . . . Zucchinis? Wait a minute! This is not suppose to be here! Go to the next one. Go to the. . . . There. Thank you.

Okay! That's more like it. This is my Uncle Al and me on opening day with our limits of pheasants. . . What's that?. . . No one took the picture. The camera has a self–timer. We set it on a hay bale. . . What's that? Our heads? That's a common occurrence with a self–timer. You don't need to see our heads to know it's us, though. Look at the shotguns! Everyone knows uncle Al and I shoot side–by–side twenties. Slide, please.

Now here's a pretty shot! Wawawai Canyon in late September—the first week of chukar season. Look at those rock formations. You can almost feel the heat. . . Pardon me? . . . No, that's my friend, Mike, in the foreground. I'm that little speck way up above the talus slope. . . Praying? No, I'm waiting for a helicopter. . . Well, actually, I'm praying for a helicopter. . . A tie? Oh, I see what you're talking about. No, Mike doesn't wear a tie when he's chukar hunting—that's his tongue. His canteen is empty—so is mine; that's why I'm praying for a helicopter. You ought to try chukar hunting sometime—it's a lot of fun when it's cool, the snakes aren't out, and someone else is doing it. Slide, please.

Whoops! Got one in upside down. Grouse hunting, I think. If you kinda lean down like this, you can make it out, though. . . A little further. . . Don't get your head too close to the cat!. . . Ouch. That must smart. I shoulda said something sooner. She's a feisty one. . . We'll just go to the next slide. Hold on a second, though, and I'll get you a Band Aid. Try not to get any blood on the couch. . . There you go. Doesn't look that serious. She bit one of the dogs a couple years ago and his head swelled up like a melon. Couldn't even open his mouth. Vet said cat bites are the worst. Okay, let's see what we have next. . . Hmmm. . . This was a lot better picture when I first took it. Don't know why Ed got so fuzzy. I think that's a blue grouse he's holding there, but it might be his underwear. Ed has this tendency for heat rash, see, and he's always putting on clean socks and. . . . Well, never mind. Let's try the next one.

Now, ya gotta love a picture like this! Turkey hunting. See that brown lump that looks like a stump?. . . Well, that's Ed again. . . No, *that* brown lump *is* a stump. I'm talking about the stump with the shotgun. . . You don't see it?. . . Why, it's right here in. . . . Hmmmm. Now, why would I take a picture of a brown stump? Slide, please. . . I said, slide, please!

Hey, you gotta stay awake, buddy. You might miss something. . . Your face bothering you?. . . Okay, okay, I'll admit you haven't missed much so far, but it gets better. This slide, for example, is one of my friend Mike on point. Look at that! Foot cocked, head forward—leaning right into it. . . What?. . . Well, I don't think it's funny at all. How you ever going to train a pup to start pointing if you don't show him what you want? Now his retrieving lessons are funny! Mike's offered me some big bucks not to show *those* pictures. Slide, please.

I took this one last September when my wife, Lacey, and I hunted doves over on Dorsal Whitney's Red Angus Ranch. You probably know the place—just out of Harrington on the other side of the cemetery. Lacey wanted me to take her picture with Dorsal's blue ribbon heifer. Lacey's the one on the right, heh, heh. Slide, please. . . I said, slide, please. . . I said. . . . Hey, get the lights, willya? Oh, dear! I mean, hello, dear! Haven't seen my projectionist, have you?. . . He left?. . . You don't say!. . . In a hurry? Did you wish him a merry Christmas? We had just been talking, dear, about that expensive suade Christmas present at the Bon Marche—the one you've been admiring since last January. Did you want that in natural or black?

Catch and (sob) release

Though I'm not above filling a stringer with enough perch or trout for a meal, I don't do it often because I'm now in my compensation phase of angling. There was a time way back in my single–digit years when I kept everything silly enough to inhale my bait, and I distinctly (and with embarrassment) remember stretching small rainbows to get them over the six–inch legal minimum. I imagine they would have raised at least a couple eyebrows had a game warden come by: trout with normal–sized heads and tails and pencil–thin bodies are not commonly found in the waters of my state.

Because I now live on a lake where the angling ranges from good to phenomenal, I have for many years fished under a set of self–imposed guidelines. If I already have fish in the freezer, I release everything lip–hooked, and I encourage the kids who hang around the community dock to try catch and release also, just to see how it feels. I understand, however, that youthful exuberance and primitive human tendencies to gather, hoard, and boast make this traumatic for some, and it is not a drum I beat too loudly. Usually, I try to teach by example, but sometimes I talk too much while I'm doing it.

To date, my largest bass weighed four pounds seven ounces, small by southern standards but pretty darn good for a cold northern lake. Around here, a largemouth over six pounds usually ends up at the taxidermist's, and I would gladly forfeit any number of left or right body parts to catch one that size. Above my fireplace is a very conspicuous empty spot between a couple whitetail racks that has been waiting many years for a six–pounder.

I wasn't as interested in fishing as I was in having an excuse to not do what I was supposed to. When I got home from work on Monday, the sun was still warm, the grebes on the lake were squalling their obnoxious/seductive mating calls, and the lily pads in front of my house were just starting to poke their shiny leaves above the surface. It was much too lovely outdoors to repaint the picnic table or clean the chimney—chores I had been avoiding with increasing guilt for weeks. Instinctively, I grabbed my spinning rod off the deck, and the next thing I knew, I was sitting in a lawn chair on the community dock, dangling a jig and wondering how I got there.

Evidently, fishing hadn't been great, for there was a lot of excitement when I immediately hooked a small trout, and a great deal more when I prepared to release it. From the far end of the dock, a youth of about 10 scrambled toward me.

"You're not lettin' that fish go, are you mister?" he asked.

"Yeah, I am."

"How come?" he asked. "Is there somethin' the matter with it?"

"I've already got fish in the freezer," I told him. "This rainbow needs to grow up a bit. You don't have to keep them to say you caught them you know." That seemed to satisfy him, and after the customary questions about lure and depth, he skipped optimistically back to his spot on the other end of the dock. No sooner had he settled down to fish again, however, than I had another strike.

"That's a bigger one," the kid squealed when the foot–long trout flashed between boat slips, zipped under the dock, and jumped on the opposite side. "You're not goin' to let that one go, are you?"

"It doesn't matter how big they are," I patiently explained

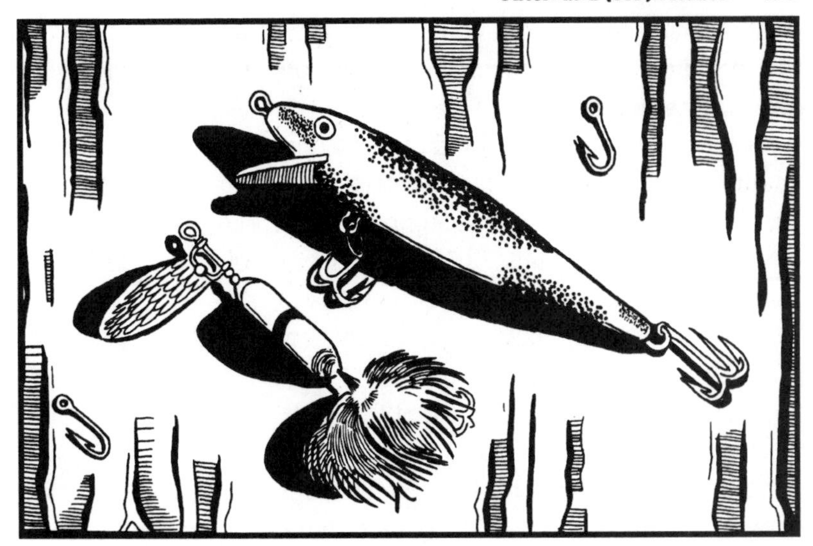

to him. "I'm not keeping any today." I smiled smugly, noting the effect of this communication, remembering how I would have reacted at the same age.

"I'll take that fish if you don't want it, mister," he said shyly as the fish thrashed the surface below us. "I been sittin' out here an hour, and I haven't caught nothin'."

"Now you wouldn't really feel very good about that, would you?" I asked, sliding my hand down the line to the hook. "A sportsman like you would rather catch his own, wouldn't he?" The hook was out, and the bright fish angled down and out of sight. The boy gave me a long, puzzled stare and walked back to his spot, shuffling his tennis shoes on the weathered planks.

The next two trout were larger still, and then I took a real beauty—a brown of almost 20 inches. Each time, the boy made the pilgrimage to stand beside me as I released the fish. Pretty soon he was telling all the after–dinner anglers—mostly children who had wandered out for an hour of fishing—about "that guy over there with the whiskers" who was releasing everything he caught. Consequently, every time I had even a nibble, I was surrounded by a half–dozen kids.

"He never keeps any of 'em," I heard the boy inform the crowd. "He said he was throwin' everything back. Said he wouldn't even keep a 10–pounder 'cause he already caught one that big once." I loved it. It's not often one gets to be a hero after the age of 40.

I knew I had a really good fish the minute it hit, but I've caught big trout, so I played it carelessly with one hand, letting the line cut the water on its long runs while I nonchalantly conversed with my fans. "It's a nice one," I told no one in particular. "Probably over five pounds."

"And you're gonna let it go—right, mister?" the boy said.

"Right," I said smiling.

"Even if it's ten pounds, right?"

"Even if it's ten pounds," I affirmed.

Had I known what I'd hooked, I would have been too excited to finesse it out of the cables anchoring the dock to the bottom of the lake. As it was, I played the big fish to near exhaustion while it was deep, then led it in. Not until its back broke the surface did I see what I had done.

"Holy criminy!" the boy gasped when he saw it. "That ain't no trout. What is it, mister?" He was on his knees, staring at the blocky, potbellied fish as it worked to stay upright, and when I didn't answer, he looked up at me in wonder. What *is* that, mister?" he repeated.

Eight pounds. Seven, anyway. It was the biggest live bass I had ever seen. My eyes glazed, and my legs began to twitch as I rose trancelike from the lawn chair, kicked a jar of salmon eggs into the water, and crunched someone's bobber under my foot. Only vaguely aware of the growing murmurs of disbelief behind me, I shakily knelt before the monstrous largemouth just as a boy of about seven made a wild stab at it with an undersized net. "Get away from there!" I ordered sharply, waving him back. The tip of the hook had barely penetrated her jaw, and I knew one more flop would set her free. I eased my hand toward her lower lip.

"Well, he aint gonna let that one go," the seven–year–old said with authority.

"Is so."

I turned my head to stare at my ten–year–old fan and the grin that girdled his face. "Is so," he said again. He jerked around to confront the crowd behind me. "He lets 'em all go," he told them innocently. "You don't have to keep 'em to have a good time, right mister?"

I glared at him dumbly. The biggest bass I had ever caught. The wallhanger I'd been looking for all those years. No way would I let this one go.

"I'll take that fish if you don't want him, mister," the seven–year–old said, rising from his knees.

"Now you wouldn't feel good about that, Jason," the ten–year–old interrupted. "Wouldn't you rather catch your own?"

"No," Jason said honestly.

"Well, I would," the ten–year–old said. "And if he lets that one go, maybe someday I'll catch him. And you know what, Jason?" he added. "I'd let him go, too, and maybe someday you can catch him."

No way would I let this one go. No way would I let this one go. No way. . . . With trembling fingers, I reached out and gave the jig a little tug. There was no splash, not even a swirl. The big female, without perceptible movement of tail or fins, simply disappeared. Perhaps she had not been there at all. Everyone groaned.

"See?" my child–fan said. "I told you. He's a sportsman, right, mister?"

I rose slowly, picked up my upended chair, folded it, gathered my gear, and, without speaking, trudged down the dock toward shore. I didn't know if I was a sportsman or not. In my mind, I had killed that fish. In my mind, it hung above my fireplace.

"Will ya be here tomorrow?" the ten–year–old called. His voice rattled around inside me for several steps.

"Not tomorrow, kid," I finally said, raising an arm in salute but not turning. "Maybe Thursday." It would take me at least a couple days to sort this one out.

About the author

Although Alan Walter Liere decribes himself as "an avid outdoor enthusiast," his wife says "zealot" is closer to the truth. More specifically, he is a trainer of wet puppies, a creator of smoky campfires, a hoarder of old fishing tackle, and a builder of fragile marsh blinds. Graduated from Eastern Washington University, first with a BA in Education and later an MA in non-fiction writing, Liere has been an English teacher in the Mead School District for the past 26 years He is a regular humor columnist for Wing and Shot, Wildfowl, and Bass 'n Gal magazines, and has published hundreds of articles in several dozen other outdoor magazines. He has received numerous national awards for his short story writing, and is the author of Bear Heads and Fish Tales, a collection of humorous essays about Alaska.

About the artist

A 20-year-old native of Portland, Oregon, A.J. Weir has lived in Spokane, Washington, the past nine years. He graduated from Mead High School in 1995 and is currently attending Cornish College of the Arts in Seattle. A versatile artist, A.J. is interested in someday illustrating a children's book, but he also aspires to eventually creating "the most elaborate pencil drawing ever seen."

To order more copies of this book:

Send $17.95 post paid (U.S. funds) check or money order per copy to:

Pease Mountain Publications
P.O. Box 216
Deer Park, WA 99006

For personalized, autographed copies, include name of recipient.